The Art of International Negotiation

The Art Of International Negotiation

Frederick Posses J.D.

BUSINESS BOOKS
COMMUNICA - EUROPA

This Edition first published in 1978 by
Business Books Ltd
24 Highbury Crescent, London N5 1RX

ISBN 0 220 663157

Typesetting by TNR Productions Ltd. London

Printed in Great Britain
by Thomson Litho Ltd, East Kilbride, Scotland

To Jevutchka *without whose encouragement this little book would not have been written.*

Contents

Preface

Why look abroad?

Perhaps in an economic Erewhon domestic markets would reflect a classically ideal balance between supply and demand, so that production and distribution would mesh and match perfectly. Cheap rawstuffs, adequate manpower, harmonious union-management relations, non-competitive merchandising, limitless funds to meet operating costs and replace obsolescent plant, machinery and tools with the latest technology, and, in consequence, a constantly increasing profit reflecting itself in an ever-rising price/earnings ratio would be the order of the day.

But economic reality consists of indefatigable cut-throat competition; tariffs are obstructive; money is dear; labour is intransigent, inefficient and indifferent to the consequences of its self-concern; energy sources are in short supply — and costly; taxation pre-empts profitability; inflation is rocketing upward and currency values are plummeting downward; share-of-the-market certainty is evanescent; and hope for restoration of economic buoyancy in domestic enterprise diminishes daily.

Home companies take a long look at the view abroad and see greener fields, greater opportunity to return to normality. Their struggle to overcome economic adversity compels them to undertake engagements in foreign business. Each company's determination to recoup its losses mirrors a particular area of unsatisfactory frustration of expectations of profitability. Each decision to open international negotiations abroad is proof that adequate alternatives do not exist in home markets. Boardroom justifications vary with the company, but they all stem from basic economic necessity. For there can be no doubt that long-distance trade on foreign soil, subject to foreign customs, usages, law, language and permutations of uncertainty, involves greater risks than those met in home markets.

Consequently, when the home company agrees to initiate international business through an international negotiator entrusted with the authority and power to commit the capital of his principal, his first duty is to ensure his mission's safety. And to this end, his point of departure lies in an understanding of his capacity, his function, and his objectives — and, urgently, the requisite negotiating strategy and tactics. He must prepare himself on a broader plane, one that will educate him to the implications of the management's decision to go abroad. Basically, of course, he should have a sufficient grasp of company policy so that his negotiating brief will conform to it. Insofar as this policy emerges from an obvious condition of necessity, the negotiator ought to familiarize himself with the particular kind of necessity compelling his company to contemplate and enter upon foreign business. Some of the common reasons for doing so are noted below. Each of them entails a knowledge of much more than the basic principles of successful persuasion. Undoubtedly each negotiator can draw on his own experience to add to the following list of economic needs leading to international negotiation:

Needs

1. Raw materials
2. Manual, semi-skilled or skilled labour
3. Reduction of operational costs
4. Counter-balance depreciating currency values
5. Offset adverse governmental fiscal regulations
6. Rationalization of production and distribution
7. Replace plant, machines and tools, methodology
8. Increase cash flow
9. Corporate diversification
10. Acquire foreign currency reserves
11. Acquire foreign expertise and technology
12. Acquire foreign market distribution

13. Convert foreign credits into equity holdings
14. Local installations for after-sales service, inventory, warehousing, and administration
15. Research and development, dispersal to protect against industrial espionage and piracy
16. Intensification of existing operations abroad
17. Acquire outlets for surplus products
18. Arrange triangulation for commodity transactions
19. Establish pilot units for administrative systems
20. Explore multi-national and trans-national potential.

The negotiator's mission abroad requires him to know his company's situation; armed factually, he may be able to present the transaction more lucidly, logically and convincingly. Even more, by exhibiting a conversance with the background materials, he can place himself at better advantage with his foreign adversary who already has an edge because of the territorial imperative. Everyone knows how much stronger one is on home ground, and how much more effectively one can marshall forces for defense and counterattack. This is emphatically true abroad where the 'playing field' is unfamiliar, and with it the culture, the language and the customs of the adversary.

It will be helpful for the negotiator to envisage his foreign transaction as comprising three integrated stages:

1. *Opening stage,* entailing an initiation of communications, a positive expression of interest in doing business, and a presentation of proposals and new offers.

II. *Middle stage,* referring to receipt, analysis and reply to new offers; definition of terms of reference within the frame of the negotiation; preparation, submission and exchange of modifications, leading to:

III. *Final stage,* describing the probable areas for agreement, eliminating non-negotiable elements, resolution of transactional terms and conditions, agreement on legal consequences, rights and remedies, and, lastly, preparation and execution of main and subsidiary instruments and documentation.

The development of our discussion will permit these stages to fall into place. For the moment, it is enough to suggest that although they are simple and logical in themselves, each stage reached abroad becomes increasingly sensitive because the negotiator must continually, and progressively, adjust himself to the possibilities of error in passing the cultural distinctions, the behavioural ambiguities, the local customs and usages and, of course, the legal restraints operative in the foreign country. As if these were not challenging enough, he has also to surmount the obstacles arising from a strange language.

For the negotiator to come through to success, his preparations should enable him to operate in two climates simultaneously, his own and that of his opposite number. If he can do so throughout the transaction, then he will minimize the likelihood of mistake and misunderstanding, either unilateral or bilateral. Once on secure terms of personal understanding with his adversary, the negotiator's approach to a meeting of the minds will present a surer prospect of success, particularly if he assimilates all of the factual material and fresh information made available to him during the bargaining process and previously, when his company first asked the question 'Why not look abroad?'

Who is an international negotiator?

It is likely that the reader is or shortly will be in some foreign business transaction requiring his participation. Were it not so, he hardly would be concerned with this discussion.

If, as may be suspected, the reader sees himself as an international negotiator, he already is a pace ahead. For business abroad, however routine, tests one's self-confidence. And whether the transaction is the first or fifty-first to be done, it searches the negotiator's self-appraisal. After all, his company's commitments lie within his hands and depend on his ability to make them intelligently, successfully and profitably. He is, to all intents, the company for so long as he is abroad.

Granting that he will have done his homework, the ideal negotiator can be anyone who is imaginative, level-headed, equable, tactful, patient, persistent and adaptable. Such a person obviously would do well in any circumstance. Such a person would have no difficulty in negotiating abroad on any plane; socially, diplomatically, commercially. Surprisingly, almost anyone possesses these attributes. They vary in kind and depth of course, but it is nevertheless true that each of us, with greater or less effort, can present himself and his purpose within a foreign milieu attractively. In a large sense, this is precisely what most of us do every day at our desk or when in the field. International negotiation demands our flexibility and diligence in conducting personal accommodations with strangers; and a foreign negotiator, if one subtracts his foreignness, is like a domestic counterpart. The makeup of either a foreign or domestic negotiator encourages what, these days, is designated as inter-personal exchange or interaction.

Everyone in industry, commerce, finance and trade will have stored up a history of give-and-take that can only benefit his efforts abroad. The great thing is to utilize experience in a rational way, embroider it with a sense of discretion, and enclose it with an appreciation of life's limitations and human frailty. On the objective side, the international negotiator may advantage himself with an ability to (a) analyze problems and synthesize responses; and (b) to swim in an ambience of foreignness, without being submerged by all the differences to be met in an alien country.

This discussion refers to no academic citations of authorities because, candidly, academic manuals could not be valid for everyone. What you can do congenially, Mr A would find awkward, and he would have to adopt another approach. We take up international negotiation as personal art. Our observations are based on personal perspectives. 'Real-life' situations abroad do not submit themselves to any pat formula.

What we do attempt to do is to sketch out the basic preparations that lend themselves to the reader's 'real-life' position abroad. We indicate something of use in forming techniques of negotiation that, plainly, would have to be tailored to suit the particular individual. Style and flair are noted as assets; each negotiator can capitalize on his own persona. His character will form his style and flair. Imitating someone else may work in one transaction, and not in any other. The international negotiation requires a sense of caution because there is something different, new, untried in every transaction; and it is the responsibility of the negotiator to sense the division between what he knows and what he is yet to learn, and then adapt his style and flair to the new occasion.

Obviously, if one can take a look at oneself, common sense points out one's weak points — which should be suppressed, and strong ones which should be emphasized.

There is sometimes a tendency to assume that foreigners, merely because they are foreigners, are uncritical of the visitor, or, if they do notice him, they do not discern him for what he is. The contrary is true; not only does the foreign negotiator see and understand keenly all that the visiting negotiator is and represents, but he measures him — against foreign standards. In fact, the truth is that the negotiator going abroad will be constantly under surveillance and critique; from the moment he dismounts to the moment he departs, everything he says and does, as well as what he does not say, will pass under hypercritical evaluation. Not only must the negotiator watch his step abroad, he must be aware that everyone else there will be summing him up, step by step. This should not deter him. After all, his first and foremost task as a persuader is to draw attention to himself, to interest his audience, to gain a receptive ear. In this light, he should remember to put on a good show until the deal is done.

Chapter 1

What internationality implies

An introduction to culture, law, politics and people abroad

Internationality tends to be polarized by us. On one hand we dismiss it as something, whatever it may be, as different and hence uninteresting to — or beneath — us. On the other, we are not beyond making a fetish of foreignness, giving marks of excellence to differences abroad whether or not they are earned by true merit. However, internationality as it applies to business negotiations especially, must be seen as a conditioning process — not unlike the algebraic problem of solving for the unknown quantum. Once the solution is reached, the problem is done. Similarly, the problem of internationality is settled once the negotiation is complete. There is no need to search out esoteric peculiarities. The negotiator need not exceed the purpose or the requirements of his brief.

So far so good. But, withal, the negotiator must come into contact, even for the moment, with things strange and confusing; so he is under a duty to see, comprehend and deal with the large features of foreignness. Should he choose to engross himself further, that is his prerogative.

Culture

We habitually separate our world into the familiar and confrontable on one side, and the strange and awkward on the other, and in doing so we are precisely following what the foreigners do. Here and abroad, however dissimulated, strangeness and unfamiliarity is equated to hostility — and is met with a like hostility. Of course this reciprocating 'enmity' rests in a primitive fear of the unknown. How shall it be treated so that we can move ahead in our business when we are in a distant land?

At the start, we know that in our own comings and goings we at home search for points of identification; and these points really are points of **identity.** Our query is 'How like me is he?'. We look at our domestic negotiating adversaries and count off how they resemble us and we them. When a sufficiency of identity is found, we talk business. We gravitate toward similarities and are repelled by dissimilarities. Knowing this, each negotiation at home entails a deliberate effort to find community of interest leading to community of endeavour in aid of community of purpose. We canvass carefully for what used to be called, more or less imaginatively, elective affinities. More prosaically, we marshall our instincts and intuitions to form first impressions of oneness, binding the other side to us. There always has been respectable authority for playing a 'hunch', for relying on one person and mistrusting another, merely because of a detail not of consequence in itself, but, by our standards and values, of much importance. Its presence turns us toward or away. Carried to some limits, this elegant, intangible, emotional sensor is a vehicle for prejudice. And this is something the international negotiator has to watch out for. He simply cannot allow preconceived bias to call the shots. He cannot go abroad with preconceptions and blind himself to cultural realities that are foreign — but valid *in situ.* Having said this, nothing more need be noted. Certainly, the negotiator's emotional response is useful; but it should be left free to function in answer to the foreign stimuli, rather than limp on the crippled leg of pre-judgement.

Of course, differences raise defenses; they do so for the reason that, as we agree, differences are joined often enough to danger. What the negotiator must accept is that the defenses he raises on first impressions are akin to those warding him off. So if he falls victim to prejudice, he must allow the same foible to his opponent — and, if this is the case, what are the chances for good foreign negotiation when both parties circle each other like alley cats?

One justification for wariness may be properly urged. Familiarity furnishes us with a standard of credibility. It is easier to accept and believe a statement made by someone known than to swallow it on the authority of a stranger, and here is where cultural influence comes into play. For, if we know a person, know from where he comes, know what he represents, then we reduce the risk of unpleasant surprise, sad disappointment, and injury. Having accepted this, the negotiator must accept as well the cultural diffidence which he will meet abroad. For foreigners hold the same views of strangers, trust, and credibility, but are determined by their cultural climate. Here, we must iterate the point for its importance: culture and transactional amicability are interlinked very substantially. We at home take identity of interest as a kind of guarantee against deceit; so do foreigners. Our version of tail-wagging holds us safe; according to our experience, we scout out the opposition before we do business with him — and the object of our tentative sniffings is to find sameness, culturally, personally if possible; our safari abroad must also measure cultural factors — but from a different aspect.

At home, we add up the positive values and then decide whether or not to negotiate, or how far to negotiate. Surface amity is a screen against the abrasions of rough and tumble commercial in-fighting. It also keeps the negotiating door open for new business.

But on foreign soil, akin to our need to assure ourselves of reliability at home, we make a canvass again; however it is precisely opposite to the domestic one. We search out cultural unlikenesses. We reason that the clime is different, therefore the cultural features should be different. If we find them so, then we inch ahead and dissect them so — finally concluding 'yea' or 'nay' on the question of whether and how to negotiate with the foreigner.

Abroad, our enquiry runs along two lines. First, we reconnoitre the general terrain, noting its gross and important character in a cultural sense. Then, having formed a view of the place and its features, we examine our adversary for proofs that he represents the cultural pattern. Now very often negotiators make a mistake. They are pleased that the foreign negotiator is so palpably like themselves in speech, poise and apparent taste. They shouldn't be, because he is concealing himself while flattering them that they are in tune with each other. They would be far better off discovering early on that he is the exact product of his culture — for then, knowing something of his culture, it would be easier to weigh him, sound him out, and close with him. The mistake is made because negotiators away from home fear being treated as they are, that is to say as strangers — which in truth they are, and in truth are so regarded. Otherwise stated, the negotiators want to be greeted as honoured guests, and are often careless enough to be put off guard by superficial adulation.

Not knowing the local customs, they confuse themselves and fall prey to the belief that they are as important as their foreign acquaintances tell them they are. And they forget to look for dissimilarities. For, abroad, it is the points of distinct differences that must be reckoned. The reason is clear enough. At home we practice psychological avoidance to overcome hostility. But abroad we must tangle with the other side; and this means that we have to gauge his strength and disposition to use it to our disadvantage. The only way to do it, to measure him, to sum him up is by tallying how he differs from us culturally.

There is a sound purpose to settling this account of negative qualities. For each of them comprises in itself a point of resistance to our approaches. And until we know the dimensions and nature of these points we cannot possibly hope to negotiate persuasively. To negotiate persuasively we must condition our adversary. And to this end we must test our power to induce him to do or refrain from doing something. Unless we know what he is made of culturally, we cannot know what he will offer by way of opposition — nor can we guess at his susceptibilities. In short, we must agree that indenticality is useful at home, and simple incongruity abroad, so far as striking a bargain is concerned.

In practical terms this implies that while a casual bonhomie is a useful lever at home with which to make an overture toward doing business, it may be ill-suited within the context of the foreign culture. And, in turn, this makes it useful — if not totally indispensable — that we start our foreign negotiation by orientating ourselves to the foreign culture. Abroad there can be no presumption of spontaneous and eternal friendliness on first sight. It simply is not intelligent on our part to let ourselves be lulled and gulled by outward show. Also, we must remember that we are under close and frequently cynical scrutiny.

Our job is to get under the negotiating skin of our adversary; and the only way to do so is by knowing him in relation to his culture. And the only way to appraise his culture is to take into account its regularities, irregularities, disjunctive features — and, again, its dissimilarities to our own. This now takes us to the key question: 'What is culture?'. The answer might surprise the reader who hitherto has glanced at the word and assured himself that culture is synonymous with aesthetic refinement. On the contrary, the true implication of culture is that it holds out the means by which a people has overcome the adversities of environment, the assaults of enemies, and the assorted ills and catastrophes of nature. By examining a culture, even in its broadest features one comes upon the inner strengths that defended the family, clan, tribe or people against extinction. By parallel reasoning, in knowing the culture abroad one knows the kind of opposition or acquiesence to be expected — and from that information it is but a step to inferring what will induce the foreign negotiator to come to agreement. In this sense knowledge is negotiating power of a sort that is indispensable. In other words it is useless for the negotiator on the verge of a foreign trip to indulge himself in the fiction of instant friendliness. This does not mean that he must not be polite. What it does mean is that he should understand how the foreigners view courtesy — and how broad is their latitude of accommodation.

To capitulate: international negotiation overtures proceed on a basis of differences sought, discovered and appraised; this is diametrically opposite to domestic negotiations, and at once requires the negotiator to safeguard his judgment against deceptive cultural similarities.abroad. On foreign soil alienation is natural, and if treated correctly can be the precursor to coming to contract. 'Coming to contract' itself entails a finding-out process. The negotiator must be able to see clearly what the other side needs, what it is willing to pay in order to satisfy its needs, and how the payments are to be made — or if defaulted, how the proposed contract can be enforced. The clue to such a fact determination lies wholly and solely in a correct assessment of the foreign culture.

If the negotiator has walked on solid ground, then he will

have no difficulty in reaching his objectives, and sealing the contract appropriately, whether it be by a striking of hands, smoking a peace pipe, or signing a contract in quadruplicate.

For example, in transacting business with the USSR or any Eastern Bloc country, it is of first importance for the negotiator to appreciate the Slavic cultural fixation on self-denial. The state comes first, least and always. This is historically valid and currently irrefutable.

Pragmatically, the force of this observation is that, allowing for human frailty, personal inducements, gifts, sweet talk, offers of eternal friendship simply do not count for much with, let us say, a Soviet negotiator, and it would be a waste of time to proceed on that line with him. Even worse, he would, by negative inference, be able to see how susceptible we are to being misled through acceptance of the very things we propose to give. In short, charisma and openhandedness are ineffectual. The first is like dropping water on stone, and the second is an invitation to disaster. Speaking generally, the case is otherwise when negotiating with the Italians, the Spanish, the French. A show of cordiality and personal concern goes a long way; and, if seen as 'sincere' can promote all kinds of modifications and accessions. Not, mind you, that these foreigners are soft-headed; rather, they are in possession of limitations that may be bent a little in the right direction when a reason exists for doing so — and what better reason can there be than a particular *entente cordiale* springing from a proper display of good will.

Incidentally, it might be noted that whatever the character of the cultural opposition, the negotiator abroad must be successful in opening, establishing and maintaining a line of communications along which the flow of offer/acceptance proposals will proceed unimpeded. With the Slavic negotiators, this can be done formally and meticulously, with Latin ones the personal involvement is sure-fire. The former would eschew anything touching on self-interest, especially because they are strictly controlled. The latter would be offended if the transaction were not set on personal rails.

This is not intended to imply that the Socialists are paragons of personal virtue and probity, as opposed to others. But they are **strictly** accountable; and their operations hold them out as agents of a state organization wherein quotes, terms and conditions are severely supervised by continuing checks and counter-checks. To vary from the strict quota or negotiating line is not only economic heresy but subject to reprimand — or worse.

However, it remains for the negotiator to school himself in the necessities of negotiating abroad on a platform of accurate knowledge. In this sense, 'know your enemy' is good advice to be considered from start to finish.

Law

From the moment that a company decides to do business abroad it comes face to face with international law. Although the concept of a universal 'law' is not strictly true, in a general sense, as it applies to common markets for example, international law holds valid. More particularly, however, international legal questions concern the impact of the law of several nations. Thus, when a negotiation brings together a French seller and an African purchaser the applicability of law must take into account both the French and the African regulatory statutes and decisions to the extent that the transaction may be governed by them.

This places the negotiator on notice that due care is required in order to ensure the legality of his proposed agreement; and this means in practical terms that it must not be put into a form that violates either country's legal concepts or procedures. Obviously, the direct way to deal with the matter is to consult a competent legal opinion.

Unless the negotiator possesses a sufficient knowledge of the applicable law, he ought to avoid 'self-help' from the outset. He cannot close his eyes to the probable risk attached to a negotiation made in contravention of relevant law. To do so is a disservice to his company and himself.

Sometimes international negotiators take it as a loss of face if they resort to professional legal advice. They believe that to receive legal advice in advance of a transaction impugnes their own sufficiency as business men. The contrary is true. Prudence dictates caution not only in moulding the substance of an international agreement in pursuit of profit, but in doing so that it does not raise later entanglements — this is emphatically true for legal questions that might have been safely put to rest if faced timely.

Another objection by negotiators must be noted. They subscribe to the view that business should be done by business men, and that legal intervention merely causes delay at best — or, at worst, destroys the intended contract by pettifoggery. Admittedly, lawyers act defensively, but they must do so in order to protect their clients. And if the intended contract cannot be drawn in conformity with the applicable law, or if it will not survive an attack, or it is not capable of enforcement, what good purpose is served by ducking the imperfections that might have been detected by counsel?

The answer to the objection should be found by the negotiator in his ability to come to agreement with a weather eye on legal practicability. Let him organize a negotiating technique that makes allowance for legal supervision, with sufficient flexibility to provide escape clauses or appropriate modifications of irregularities so that, in the end, legality may be assured. It would be foolhardy to enter a foreign negotiation and take it to the penultimate stage, just before the documents are to be executed, only to meet with meritorious legal objections at the critical moment. Returning the negotiation to square one at such a point must inevitably sour the transaction. And the responsibility for doing so lies at the door of the negotiator, not the lawyer. Common sense recommends due caution be taken legally well in advance of the journey abroad. Like all generalities, this advice is open to exception — as, often enough, some opportunities cannot 'wait' for legal certainty. Nevertheless, even in exceptional transactions, a skilled negotiator will know how to settle the business side while reserving for final legal approval all of the questions that could infringe upon his company's rights and interests. Like traffic control, legality is meant to protect the road users against mishap. And, like traffic accidents, contractual misadventures are often encouraged by those who disregard the plain necessity for exercising due care.

Returning to the international negotiator's outlook, it can be stated positively, that if he wishes to be successful he must accept the fact that foreign countries, within their own cultura! evolution, have evolved laws for the control of their interests that, although different from his own, aim at themes with which he should be conversant. Therefore, it is only reasonable for him to imagine the existence abroad of statutes, decisions and legal practices that enfold, amongst other things, the making of a contract, the conditions for its enforcement, the impact of tariffs and taxation, the limitations of patentability and copyright, the imposition of currency controls, the relations between unions and management, the state's view of warranties and manufacturer's liability, trade descriptions, employer's duties relative to workmen's compensation, relevant social welfare provisos, export/import permits, and thousands of other details that touch the conduct of industry, commerce, trade and finance. The very moment that the negotiation walks on foreign soil, it brushes against legal questions that search for legal answers. Whether the issue raised is one of performance or payment, extra-territoriality or internal legal precedence, it should be examined, considered and carried to the company lawyer for an opinion before the foreign business is consummated in a contract. Again, it is no loss of face for the negotiator to do so. He need only pause a moment and remember that within his own country, every day, in a multitude of tribunals, in a plethora of arbitration hearings, matters of business are being determined because of legal complications — of which many could have been avoided if submitted for a consultative opinion in good time.

A passing note on extra-territoriality might not be amiss. In essence the principle relates to the reach of our own government beyond the national frontiers. This reach covers our company in some ways, and in other ways it takes hold of us as individuals. The effect of extra-territorial interest continues even when we are thousands of miles away from home. So, familiarly, mere absence from home does not exclude or shield us from military service; nor does it exempt our company from tax liabilities. Of course the extra-territoriality can be a blessing — as when we are run afoul of some foreign law, we take to consular intervention on our behalf. Again, when our company's foreign-based factory becomes nationalised suddenly by some other nation, it turns to our government to seek assistance in gaining redress.

The exercise of favourable extra-territorial intervention on behalf of ourselves or our company is always subject to the conditions of the particular nation wherein we, or our company, may be at a disadvantage. Thus, our government's action in China would be vastly different from what it might be in Zaire. It is up to the international negotiator, before he travels out to a foreign country, to consider how extra-territoriality will work its effects for him and his company in the event of need. Such contemplation in advance is wise and should not be dismissed out of hand.

Narrowing our focus on legality, it is important to accept that the original body of the law (*corpus juris*) has become changed by politics and economics so that, for the purposes of international negotiation, the common market communities must be seen as adding to the *corpus juris* regulatory decisions that run across the national frontiers of their members. Simply stated, in doing business in France, the negotiator will be wise to have not only a conspectus of the applicable French law, but also that of the EEC tribunal decrees. In addition, there are determinations made by the separate committees of the EEC to which attention should be given. Here, again, it is ordinary good practice to explore the legal ground abroad before negotiating. So, where the negotiator is sent abroad for the purpose of dealing in strategic minerals, he would serve his company well by absorbing some knowledge of the foreign government's controls over strategic minerals; and in the case of an EEC country he could not do better than enquiring into all of the applicable regulations covering the sale and purchase of such materials.

So far, we have mentioned the reluctant negotiators who for one cause or another hesitate to take legal advice. There is another side of the coin to be mentioned. There are business men who are content to thrust upon their attorneys the full weight of the business to be done. 'Leave it to our lawyers', they say. As a tribute to the legal profession, such a gesture is welcome. But it is not always sensible *per se*; lawyers in general practice are useful for their view-in-the-round. When they perceive that a specialist would be required, they are ready to go farther and recommend one. Certainly they have a generalist's outlook that comprehends various phases of a transaction. Yet they ought not to be burdened with the hypertechnicalities of a commercial venture. These matters are for businessmen, and should remain so.

International lawyers, as such, are equipped to take up

matters displaying a contiguous connection as between several legal systems; but this does not mean that they ought to be woven into the fabric of a decision as to the advantage or disadvantage of buying a cotton future, or setting up an oil refinery, or organizing a franchise chain. Such decisions — even where dependent on an ascertainment of applicable law — remain business judgments for businessmen.

A mundane issue as to what should be done in a foreign emergency is worth talking about. Theoretically, the law exists on a plane apart from the negotiator. He has access to a lawyer at home, or his company can provide one. But in foreign territory he may need immediate advice. Where should he turn? The problem can be resolved easily in advance. Before he goes abroad, he can ask the company lawyer (or his personal attorney) for an introduction to someone whose professional legal help can be sought, not only on company business but also for personal representation.

Thus, in addition to glancing at — or even preparing — contractual documents, the local foreign lawyer can be of great help in the event of a road accident, a dispute over hotel bills, an outright overcharge, a false accusation, bad accommodation, entrapment, police harassment, bureaucratic delay, personal injury, confiscation, excessive surveillance, espionage, and even family matters. These can mount up into a storm of embarrassment — and the need for a lawyer at once is not always satisfied by a list of lawyers in hand. The practical thing to do is to contract the company (or personal) lawyer and provide an introduction. Then, while the negotiator is at leisure after arrival, he should present himself and exchange a few words with the local lawyer. This will enable him to know upon whom he can count — and it will permit the local lawyer to determine whether he will be free to act for the negotiator. It would be inconvenient for him to do so if there were a conflict of interest situation, and it would be foolish for the negotiator to engage someone who could not be counted on to be ready, willing and able. Even more important is the fact that foreign communications are unlike those at home. Foreign 'availability' is often limited by saints' days, public holidays, and other circumstances that will delay the negotiator in extricating himself from a tricky situation. Furthermore, foreign countries do not always offer a pleasant political aspect to the negotiator — and far worse, the national or individual xenophobia abroad may be evidenced in a manner that threatens the mission, or the personal safety, of the negotiator. It's always good sense to be armed with a local legal friend. And it's always wise to assure his presence before the need for him arises.

The reader, during this discussion, may be seen as smiling in disbelief at the view that a local lawyer can be a negotiator's best friend. Nevertheless and notwithstanding his assurance, he should be well aware that a foreign market is completely different from the domestic one in this respect. At home, the market is made up, generally, of people one knows or about whom one can enquire. One's friends and competitors can be checked against all kinds of references. One can even rely on the maxim that 'The law is an ass' and eschew legal advice if one so chooses. But in foreign precincts the law, if invoked by an unfriendly rival, may become 'an ass' with a powerful kick.

At home we think of some restraints that influence fair play of a kind in our market. Abroad, the sense of fair play is absent or so distorted that we can only be astonished — or, worse, badly disadvantaged. Legal corner-cutting, illegal overreaching, personal spite, malicious and false complaints, no-holds-barred complotting and mercenary informers all operate as naturally as members of a club; indeed, in a sense they are members of a 'let-us-work-together-and-sink-the-intruder' club; the negotiator as intruder can be a target for disappointed 'intermediaries', government agents with their hands out, foreign company officials seeking to feather their nests, disgruntled opportunists. And to these may be added chance acquaintances, of one or another kind. All of them, under the cover of anonymity, for one or another reason, using any kind of pretext, can be a source of serious vexation, harassment and inconvenience to the negotiator. While 'defend yourself at all times' is a good motto, it is even more useful to be able to call on a local lawyer to assist in the defense when an emergency arises.

Legal prophylaxis, like medical prophylaxis, should be seen as helpful, preventative, indispensable, and readily accessible. The responsibility for having it available in a foreign business negotiation lies with the negotiator. It makes for efficiency, it ensures his safe arrival and departure and it provides for the normal transaction of the business upon which he goes abroad. Self-esteem, if nothing else, should urge the negotiator to support his negotiating abroad with whatever will ameliorate the bargaining climate, promote a sound contract for his company, and keep him personally free from harm.

Politics

Abroad, as at home, the form and character of government, and the nature of those who hold office or seek to hold office within it, inevitably influence the course of doing business. Whether the negotiator is directly or indirectly in the path of a political decision, he must take cognizance of it and consider as a relevant factor the impact of such a decision upon the foreign company and its inclination to negotiate. The consequences of such a decision may be immediate or deferred, vital or peripheral, concentrated on a particular facet of the negotiator's endeavours, or widespread. Whatever the case, politics in a foreign country reflect not only that country's ordinary economic policy but also the opportunity for doing whatever the negotiator's company means to do. The negotiator abroad on a transaction involving the institution of a programme to rationalize local production units can only discharge his function by estimating the results of such a programme upon the foreign community, its labour force, its unions, and its pricing structure. To do so properly, and with an informed standpoint, he should not hesitate to acquaint himself with a useful political friend, or several of them. Apart from smoothing the road to contract through official channels, such a friend can supply advance notice of beneficial or restrictive tendencies in government regulation of business and the way it is done abroad.

Whenever government approval, through one of its officials or bureaux, must be sought, then a friend at court, so to speak, is invaluable. Whatever entails permits, licenses, consents or ratifications should be foreseen and aided as much as possible through political contacts. Building plans, special export facilities, exemptions from certain taxes, zoning variances, construction of plant, procurement of transportation or warehousing accommodations — indeed, almost everything that falls within the scope of business, must be thought over with particular reference to the implication it carries. These implications will be appreciated by the local political figures in terms of their official duties; and if their duties are or may be helpfully exercised, or — conversely — if they are disinclined to act in aid of the negotiator's program, it becomes of first importance to the negotiator to establish as early as possible a friendly relationship with the official (or one of his mutual friends) whose authority can sway the official, whose power and inclination are essential.

Sometimes the appeal to the foreign official may rest on personal loyalties; at other times, it may rest on an objective demonstration that, for instance, the location of a new assembly plant, while advantageous to the negotiator's company, will be of immediate and substantial benefit to the foreign community in terms of more jobs, more per capita disposable income, more sales, better housing, improved utilities — and, derivatively, greater appreciation for the political figure whose intervention propelled the transaction toward a conclusion.

Politics and politicians may be invisible, so to speak, in their offices. But social contact can be a means of acquaintance that will open up their views and incline them to listen to those of the negotiator. This is practical, and, in one or another way, practicable.

The negotiator, for his own sake, ought to sidestep any suggestion that he himself holds a personal stake in the outsome of the transaction, or that he has a personal relationship with the official figure. The reason for this is that abroad, as at home, for every political friend one makes, there are a dozen actual or potential enemies stirred to envy and disfavour. And since the 'in' party can become the 'out' it is prudent to keep one's personal interest quiet lest one become the target of reprisal when political fortunes abroad change. This is most important for the reason that foreign politics in many countries tend to be subject to sharp reversals, upheavals, and radical retaliation for long-remembered disadvantage. The negotiator ought not to count on being treated gently as a 'stranger within the gates'. More likely he will be pinpointed as the devil, to be cast out or, much worse, subjected to some unwelcome penalty for having meddled personally in the community's internal affairs.

He should see to it that his political prescience and participation abroad are unobtrusive and unobjectionable. In a word he can afford to be politically alert but not politically involved on a personal level. If he ventures too far and makes himself politically obnoxious, his company's efforts will abort, and he will be made to bear the brunt of his personal incaution.

Having in mind what has been said with a view to keeping open the pipe-line to political connections, the key question for the negotiator is how to go about it. To begin with, his homework might include the collation of as much information as can be procured concerning the local political figures, their prejudices, their personalities, their status within the local hierarchy. All background data should be sifted for signs of favourable or adverse personal attributes. Their backgrounds should be studied so that their ambitions and prospects, or lack of them, can be evaluated.

The next thing to do is to look about for an initial contact; it can be made on an official basis, as through a consul abroad, or attendance at a chamber of commerce meeting, or through personal introduction — as, for example, might be made by one's local lawyer. Successively, to the extent necessary — and not any farther, the negotiator can open up his proposed transaction to the politico and sound him out. Assuming that the negotiator is mature and accustomed to dealing with people, he can settle on whatever else is to be done.

However the initial contact is made, whether through a local lawyer or friendly bank manager, or a company accountant, or a trade association officer, or through colleagues or social acquaintances, it is up to the negotiator to be alert to the need for 'sponsorship'. At the start, he can always use a good word in his favour. His personality will be tested soon and often. So it will serve his best interests to make his appearance under the aegis of a local who is respected and in good standing, and who will be a testimonial to his own reliability and probity.

Obviously enough, the negotiator's experience at home, where it will be assumed that he can charm the birds off the trees, should stand him in good stead here. With adequate self-confidence, an introduction under useful auspices, and armed with a proposal that can advance the interests of a political figure while benefiting the foreign community, there is no reason for the negotiator to hang back. One thing he ought to bear in mind and that is: a politician can make a good friend — or a bad enemy. If the negotiator becomes *persona non grata,* his company's standing will suffer — perhaps disproportionately. And, moreover, he must always see to it that the way home is free and clear, without ill will. It can be difficult getting out of a locked door.

People

Foreigners are people. People must be understood. The negotiator must understand them. For reasons that defy exact analysis when we go abroad we tend to regard people as curiously constituted phenomena, to be observed at a distance and marked as oddities according to their idiosyncratic behaviour. This is fair enough, since the foreigners look at us in very nearly the same way. But it does not take us far along the road to making contact.

We forget, in a foreign ambience, all of the techniques for negotiation acquired so assiduously during our years. Or, conversely, we adopt a kind of pidgin/babytalk/lingua franca that invites contempt, causes offense, and thwarts our purposes.

The strategies we mean to work, the persuasions we are about to effectuate, and the contract we seek to form are stillborn in our obduracy. What is needed by us is an appreciation that foreigners are rational, emotional and spiritual human beings. By appreciation we must understand more than complacent tolerance of strangeness. For unless we can dig into the motives of the other parties to our transaction, then there is simply no chance of convincing them that all we seek is practical, attainable and profitable to them. We need to know something of their history, something of their personalities, something of their hopes and aspirations in order to do business with them. Without such a general knowledge there can be no opportunity for us to apply psychological principles, or turn the tenets of social behaviourism to our advantage. In a word, to draw them to a position where they are 'open to buy' we should know what their make-up is, how it finds expression, and what will appeal to their interests.

This boils down to a need to know with whom we are dealing so that our communications are slanted correctly, are capable of stimulating positive responses, and are useful to our purposes. The way to do this is by taking a firm grip on bedrock understanding of what they say, how they move, what they intend through their gestures and gesticulations. When we accomplish this, then we can move on to considerations of neutralization whereby we disarm their hostility and convert them into attentive role-players. Their role, from our viewpoint, is to listen and come to agreement. All of the textbooks on psychology will be just so much dry rot unless we do what is prerequisite: swing them over to our negotiating song. As in everything else, negotiators are likely to take one of two extreme lines. Either they are 'hard-sell' specialists, and pound away at the unenlightened natives, or they wrap their contracting spiels in tortuous terminology, hoping to impress their audiences with conspicuous signals of refinement and academic elegance. In between lies a better middle road, but it is so simple that it suffers from avoidance. What the negotiator should do in a foreign country is to reduce everything to its proportions, within the language and customs of the place. What he says must be tailored to the person whom he is addressing; and that person must be spoken to without condescension, obsequiousness, or indifference. This formula presupposes that the negotiator's knowledge of his subject matter will be proof against fault-finding; that the initial proposals will invite serious consideration; that his promises are susceptible of demonstrable proof, and that his attitude is one of commensurate respect, and self-respect.

Taking the foregoing as established, it remains wholly within the discretion of the negotiator to pick the right time and place for his negotiation. Later on in our discussion we are going to supply hints on conducting foreign negotiations, and in that context we shall have something to add on communications. If anything is to be understood about the need for settling a means of persuasion, it might be stated this way: the negotiator and the foreign adversary must be taken into a position where they exchange and participate in the creation of contractual ideas. They should not be like opera singers, performing a duet back to back, neither one hearing the other, each being intent only on vocalizing his part. Negotiation is transaction; transaction implies the existence of common interest; common interest must be seen to exist, and must pervade the sense and atmosphere of all that the negotiator carries abroad with him. Unless this can be done well, he will not make the most of his company's opportunity to do foreign business. True, we are rapidly enjoying the endless and increasing blessings of computerization, electronic calculations and instant air transport. But we still need to deal with each other, native or foreign though we may be, in terms of proper people possessing individual motives, driven by individual desires — and subject to individual preferences and prejudices. The negotiator abroad, as at home, must defer to the human condition.

Chapter 2

Foreigners and foreign cultures

Culture as a behavioural influence; some cases in point; how to appreciate alien life-styles; an understanding of culture; the art of credibility; how foreigners view a foreigner; how to cope with hostility; the Eastern Bloc; the foreigner as an individual and the art of negotiation on a personal level.

International negotiations involve foreigners; to understand how the foreigners think, it is essential that we understand their cultures. To understand how they may see us, we must see them within their cultural backgrounds. This seems straightforward in theory, but it is sometimes ignored, or if not ignored, insufficient effort is made. We focus on the familiar when, in truth we are in a strange place amongst strange people. Sometimes the strangeness hits us at once. The kind of clothing the foreigners wear, the social attitudes they take, the communal structures they create, their habitual movements and manners are at odds with ours. But in most instances, the surface similarities, the general standardization of images produced by the compression of our aircraft, electronic communications and pervasive theatrical representations on television, in the cinema and over the radio misleads us into supposing 'we' and 'they' think alike and feel alike. The truth is otherwise; and deep in their consciousness their cultural differences assert themselves and lead foreigners to different interpretations of what we, among our friends at home, believe fitting, acceptable and good.

Across the foreign border, the negotiator must observe and note the alien movements carefully and distinguish them from his own in order to evaluate their positive or negative relation to the actions and responses of his foreign adversary.

Domestic companies are preoccupied with what they can produce and how they can produce, tending to neglect what the foreign market demands actually are. It is not that the laws of supply and demand are forgotten, but the domestic view of them is often through a one-way mirror preventing each side from seeing the other clearly and making allowances for local peculiarities.

A recent example makes the point. An English firm took an order for kitchen ranges to be sold in Italy. It filled the order and shipped twenty thousand units. On arrival at Genoa they were inspected and rejected because they were not fitted with connectors used in Italy; instead the connectors conformed to those suited to English homes. Had even superficial note been taken by the manufacture of the desired connectors' dimensions, the deal would have been completed as both sides originally had intended. Instead it became a controversy, and, of course, an exhibit in the history of cultural disorientation in the domestic market.

There have been cases of domestic companies sending negotiators into a foreign market with little or no briefing on foreign differences. Not a word of instruction as to how the locals do their business, or when. Even though the companies at home set their own time, fix their own place, and pick their own moment to talk business, they entirely avoid the need of conforming to foreign customs or idiosyncracies. It is not unusual for an American to blunder into Turin somewhere about 2 p.m., seeking an appointment with his opposite number in order to arrange their first conference. Anytime before the conventional lunch and siesta period, lasting until 3 p.m. could have been chosen without difficulty, had the visitor been thoughtful of what the Italian midday ritual was. For some reason not readily discernible, there seems to be a feeling that if one defers to foreigners one loses face; that, apart from obtuse disregard of everything alien, might explain but it does not justify the negotiator's blurred sight of cultural differences.

Internationality, somewhat like cosmopolitanism, should begin with an awareness of alien life styles; and it should be coupled with an acceptance of them within the climate of their ordinary incidence. History, tradition, morality, ethics, and political organization, to cite some of the points of difference, far more than territorial borders, denote foreignness. In our times, borders are obliterated by machines, communications and economic efficiency. But cultural differences remain. To be an internationalist, comfortably conducting negotiations in Alaska on Tuesday and in Zanzibar on Saturday, it is essential for the negotiator to leave his home base disposed to note and deal with the foreigners' differences. Whether he represents a seller or a purchaser, the minute he goes abroad, he ought to be ready to adapt himself to the necessities of the occasion insofar as cultural difference requires him to do so. The responsibility lies with him to conform to the foreign ways, not to attempt to change them to conform to his. This applies whether he must develop an interest in his company's new invention or lay the foundation for a consortium or promote a new after-sales service. Every venture into foreign fields places the burden of adaptation on the shoulders of the negotiator; and he cannot discharge that burden by mere lip-service to custom. To give slipshod attention to foreignness, cultural differences and local trade patterns is totally senseless.

Cultural differences must be seen as they are. Culture itself may produce exotic delights, but, as mentioned in the introduction, it is basically the sum of what people have learned in their struggle to survive. Cultural patterns evolve from the environment within which a people must discover, improvise and employ the best and most efficient ways to eat, feed and defend itself. If it hits upon reed thatching as a roof-making process, that is a cultural contribution; if it adds adornment to the thatching, that is an aesthetic advance — but still rooted in the need for survival, and thus seen it represents something that distinguishes one people from another. Culture is telelogical. There is a direct line between what a people needs and what it devises to supply that need. It would be imperceptive if the negotiator chose to ignore the foreign cultural ambiance because in doing so he is shutting his eyes to an economic index as well as to a patent expression of foreignness. He should go abroad prepared to hear, see, taste and feel the local atmosphere in terms of what it is rather than what, at home, he had imagined it to be. He must understand the foreigners in relation to their totality of differences. They are rooted in a different cultural matrix from his own. Unless he understands this matrix, he will prejudice his understanding of his foreign adversary. He cannot separate the adversary from his cultural predilections. There is a saying in the South of the United States, 'You can take the boy out of the country, but you can't take the country out of the boy'.

Much is made of corruption in high places abroad, and one hears of foreign officials being dismissed for having demanded bribes. Somehow the complicity of those who met the demands, if demands they were, becomes diluted by the plaint that 'everybody's doing it'. The truth is that corruption is not the invention of the foreigners and they have no monopoly on its effective uses. What is relevant, though, is that the foreign bribe runs parallel to the home grown 'inducement', and the latter is treated as a minor mistake. Without passing any moral judgment, demands, extortions, bribes, or 'inducements' are as old as the hills and are universal; but their condemnation is not. The negotiator may be faced with the need to deal with them abroad, one way or the other. Whichever path he elects to follow, it is obvious that local requirements must be respected.

The norms and standards which guide the foreigners need not influence his own ethical views and practices, but they are entitled to be noted. Despite what we have said about corruption, the failure to offer a gift to a business man can be interpreted as offensive in some parts of the world. In others, it is mandatory. In still others it is a signal offense that would halt any hope of doing business. So, the noble resolve of the negotiator while in Venezuela to eschew even the appearance of 'inducement' led him to a strict and puritanical neglect of a token of his esteem. The Venezuelan regarded the negotiator as boorish, discourteous and insultingly rude. Moreover, the Venezuelan accepted the absence of an appropriate token of esteem as a slap in the face, one that implied that he simply had no power to confer or withhold a favour, and he thereafter became 'invisible' to the negotiator, who left the Tamanaco at Caracas promptly at 7.30 a.m. and further attempts to see the Venezuelan were fruitless.

In Japan, a decorously presented gift of a pearl necklace should be taken as a graceful gesture. The gift to the negotiator's wife is an act of politeness, and so is a gift of a ball-point pen bearing the company name and address. To refuse either would be rude, and could prejudice the outcome of the negotiation abroad. English and American negotiators are not averse to using all forms of inducements which they consider ethical, for instance, club memberships, air-travel tickets, hidden rebates, leading to favourable rulings by municipal zoning boards allowing variations from building codes and property uses, are not uncommon. Culture and all of its trappings, are, for better or worse, expressions of people; and foreign cultures express foreign people. The negotiator must not be put off by foreign cultural differences. When in Rome, he may not subscribe to the local view of 'inducements', but he ought to refrain from decrying it.

To spare his anguish at outlandish cultural differences, the negotiator should orient himself to what he can expect on his foreign journey, how he might condition his reponses to them, and what to do about those that may take him out of his depth. He should remember that we look on our familiar world as friendly. Foreigners do the same in respect of their own. We regard strangeness as fearsome and dangerous. So do they. The unknown is forbidding to both sides alike. So each of us reject dissimilarity. In this we and they resemble each other. Consequently, the logical method toward a trading overture lies in first identifying and sorting foreign dissimilarities. When we do this consciously we unconsciously begin to form a rough impression of how our exchanges ought to be developed. Having a sense of what the foreign adversary will do within the framework of his cultural differences makes it easier to envisage the construction of a trading community of interest, and helps create a talking point, (or as many talking points as touch our business) of how to join forces in maturing the contract.

Sometimes we may be thrust back by an apparent indifference. It may be a cultural convention, as it is in certain Oriental countries, for the Japanese or Chinese representative to appear impassive. Whereas, in the Latin countries, the Spanish, Portuguese or South American negotiators may be volatile about apparently irrelevant matters. Here it is necessary to proceed cautiously, perhaps resorting to what formerly was called the theory of elective affinity. This can be understood as 'first impression'. We either sense a friendly bond at the initial meeting, or else the contrary reaction arises.

In other words, we exchange experience and intuitive instinct for a bond that will establish a springboard for further useful exchange.

This is not altogether nebulous if we reduce elective affinity to the more realistic search for mutual credibility. In this respect 'credibility' does not require either side to trust the other implicitly; rather, it furnishes an index as to what is believable in the character of the adversary as perceived against his cultural background. Once we ascertain this kind of credibility, we can do two things. We can speak to him within his cultural limitations; and, simultaneously, we can create at least a facsimile of friendliness that will smooth out the ordinary abrasiveness or deceit of a first meeting. That such encounter-reactions are commonplace, both in home markets and foreign ones can be frankly admitted. That they may be replaced by more productive attitudes is equally true. And so far as international matters are concerned, a tremendous stride forward to an abatement of hostility exists with an insight into the influence of culture on foreign business attitudes. In fact, if a particular foreign negotiation were to be suspended as inconclusive, a later resumption on amicable terms would be acceptable where the negotiator knew and respected his adversary's present inability or reluctance to proceed to formal contract because of an inhibition or convention rooted in local mores.

Let us consider a hypothetical negotiation with a foreign visitor who was anxious to come to firm agreement, had little time available, and was pressing for contract preparation; and suppose that the negotiator's company president had just died. What can be done but defer the contract completion for a decent interval? Long enough at least for the ceremonies to be performed and a successor to the president chosen. This would accord with his particular pattern of culture. In some foreign countries such an occasion would call for more than dutiful reverence. Perhaps a week, or a month, or even longer would be the minimum period of mourning before the resumption of negotiations. In other countries, particularly those of the Slavic or Eastern Bloc, the opposite is true. Not because of a lesser regard for the deceased, but because the cultural pattern is tied into the political organization of state agency; and when one official passes on because of death, retirement or otherwise, he is immediately replaced. This, amusingly, resembles the historical "The King is dead, Long live the King" thread of continuity known to monarchies. Dozens of examples of influential cultural oddities might be cited without altering the main point. However, the point can be highlighted by saying that while at home, in Anglo-Saxon negotiations we are regarded as substantially inclined toward congeniality, and foreigners find our culture of service-with-a-smile somewhat disconcerting. Of course they know how to smile, but they smile for reasons other than ours. Therefore, when we are met with a smile abroad we should not assume it's our kind of smile, we must instead understand it within the local cultural experience. To take it at face value would be naive, and in the long run might mislead us.

Having touched on the initial hostility, mistrust and abrasion to be expected on arriving in some foreign country, it is only right to say that prior experience of bad negotiations may have done much to confirm our adversary in his stand-offishness. A useful example might be taken from a recent transaction in which the author was engaged to go to Spain under instructions that were clear enough but, for one or another reason wholly omitted an adequate history of the transaction. When he came to the negotiation site, in place of the cordial welcome he had expected he received a frigid, indifferent greeting. During the next day or so he managed to get to the heart of the hostility and found somewhat to his dismay that his principal had defaulted on obligations already incurred with the Spaniards; that he had refused to suggest any programme for making good his default; that he sought to evade his responsibility by recourse to subterfuge; and, finally, that he had told the Spaniards that the author was fully authorized to introduce third parties into the transaction — and that the third parties were at hand with all of the funds necessary to resuscitate the now moribund hopes of the Spaniards.

The reader may well imagine the author's dilemma. Having the true state of affairs before him, he could neither criticize his Spanish hosts for their statement that they would not move an inch, nor could he dare to put forward any sugggestion of his principal's good faith. What he did was all that in the circumstances could safely be done. He drew the Spaniards to a friendlier attitude, suggested a negotiating detente, and left the door open to a resumption of dealing on a fresh relationship in the form of a reorganization of the participating interests — subject, naturally, to his principal's approval and undertaking. The terms of the undertaking were kept open, although the effect of the undertaking was intended to restore the sense of good faith now absent. Seen in this way, the cultural impact was met and dealt with.

Something must be said on the theme of how negotiators look at foreigners, and how foreigners look at them. In spite of all the broad-minded views social studies tell us we must hold of our foreign brothers, the fact is that after we set foot on foreign soil we still think of *them* as foreigners. And they resent this insufferable gall. It irks them when we, with deliberate condescension or unconscious rudeness call attention to *their* peculiarities, while overlooking rudimentary good taste. More to the point, they resent our bland attempts to explain them to themselves, and they understandably fume when we draw comparisons favourable to us.

The cultural lag is far more important than the one we sustain after a trans-Atlantic flight. It is a pity that international business often suffers needlessly in the hands of negotiators who refuse to exercise their innate wit. After all, it is so easy to learn what will please or offend one's business counterpart — and then avoid offensive speech or conduct. More practically, it makes more sense to learn what he likes or dislikes, because when we do we have a direct line into his mind and heart. We can persuade him more effectively. If we take no notice of his culture, we might just as well give up the idea of convincing him of anything we have to offer. Admittedly, if he is desperate, if we are the single resource, if we go to him — then, perhaps, we can compel him to accept our terms despite our total obtuse and unappreciative disregard of what he is, how he came to be that way, and why he must do what he does as he does it. Otherwise, given a free choice, the chances are he will see us as a plague.

Standing now at the verge of an international negotiation, we must remember what our premise was with respect to identities and differences. At home, we said, we seek to establish resemblances between ourselves and those we do business with. Abroad we do otherwise, probing for the local qualities that vary from ours. In a general way, we might even go so far as to say that some sort of ratio governs friendliness and coincidence of interest, as opposed to indifference, hostility, and the absence of mutual interest. This is only reasonable in view of our understanding that strangeness, alienation and unfamiliarity give occasion for fear — and fear itself is an expression of hostility.

The instinctive response to hostility takes us away from the source of fear. We deliberately call on what is called the psychology of avoidance. Nevertheless, since we sought out the advantages of doing business abroad, we must penetrate the local hostility, and this can be done by dispelling the local fear. And here is where the art of international negotiation must be exercised. We begin with a candid sight of ourselves as the true foreigners, for so we are seen when on foreign soil. We must appraise ourselves and uncover what excites hostility, and to what extent it influences our foreign adversary. This leads us further into a critique of his culture. For, in order to allay his fears and invite his cooperation, we must know something of his ethnic background and of his personal make-up. Only if we perceive him as he is conditioned can we perceive ourselves through his eyes.

Perceiving him signifies something more than a cursory assessment of his personality. It entails an analysis of his bargaining susceptibilities. At home we have learned how to anticipate, literally, what the man across the table will require for agreement. We fit him into a precise social category, and then measure his potential for agreement, resistance, and compromise, and this evaluation goes forward on his points of identity. In a foreign land we employ virtually the same process, but the base of our observation is that of difference, distinctiveness and distinguishable characteristics. In both cases, the results lead us to inferences of what our tactics of persuasion and the appropriate negotiating stage during which we may use them.

Sometimes the division between him and ourselves is substantial, sometimes fanciful, sometimes beyond our comprehension. Nevertheless, we do not go abroad in order to indulge ourselves in amateur psychology. We must simply construct a bridge that will take us to the series of personal connections essential to contract formation. This bridge is more than a landing site. It functions as a pivot of predictability. We are aiming at a method of determining what his movements may be, in which direction they will go, and how we can guide them towards an agreement. Here again we must account for his culture; even more, we must see the effects our culture work on him.

At home, we are acquainted with the uses of what might be described as the foreplay of friendliness. But that friendliness is held within acceptable forms. We defer to rank and privilege. We mark social signs as trail-blazers and follow them. Easy, breezy and bold bonhomie may be suitable in one circumstance but not another. And whether it is an exact calculation or 'educated intuition', we try not to overstep the barriers. Exactly the same particularity is called for when we act abroad but of course, the determination of the barriers is facilitated by common language, common concepts and common cultural preoccupations. The flow, play and interaction of ideas can be channelled discreetly; and we are ready to receive and interpret the responses to our signals. Abroad it is prerequisite for us to chart our course carefully because the culture, language, history and tradition we must deal with are vastly at variance with our own.

Take the example of our philosophy of 'doing business' by following a middle way. In our native haunts, the idea of determinedly holding on to an initial position simply does not make sense. We appreciate the prudence of middle ground negotiation and express it in the phrase 'give and take'. In some negotiations held with Belgians, the opening stages of the conferences were studded with the other side's iterated and reiterated obduracy. An insistence on 'my just rights' echoed throughout the first days. It was not until the author was able to wait out the moment for a pause that the conference could be steered to an alternative approach. Admittedly, the fresh course was not the product of inspiration. It consisted of suggesting that 'just rights' could be defined in various ways, and that, for practical purposes, they did not come to the fore until the areas of agreement were defined. By good fortune, the Belgians were amenable to the suggestion. Perhaps they had merely intended to exhibit their version of hard-nosed negotiation. In any event, the results were productive. Incidentally, having used the words 'good fortune', it is important for every international negotiator to value luck. What luck may be lies beyond clinical analysis. Some say it is being at the right place and at the right time. Even that is altogether vague — for who knows what the right time is when he is on foreign soil? Overall, luck carries far more weight than logic. One may be consistently logical and yet still fail to win a contract. On the other hand a chance word, an innocent gesture, even an idle rumour can modify favourably or ruin irredeemably the most meticulously planned business dealings.

One speaks of points of identity and similarities at home as keynotes to good transactions. Yet in another cultural milieu the very occurrence of coincidental appearances, manners and attitudes must not be accepted *prima facie* as proof of negotiating tractability on the part of the adversary. On the contrary, since they are flowing away from the mainstream of the foreign culture, they should be questioned. They may be pure artifice designed to lead the negotiator into a lax state of mind or they may be illusory and the result of his wish that everything abroad were as it is at home. They may merely be politeness itself. But however likenesses appear, because they are literally out of place, they must be treated with circumspection. Amusingly, our own assumed 'foreign' manners will be seen for what they are. We may toast our foreign colleagues in their own tongue. We may go to their bull-fights, eat their snails, pinch their geisha girls, but we remain who we are — and we shall never delude them into believing or accepting us otherwise.

The sum of our alert regard for cultural matters seems to be that we must accept foreignness when we are abroad, and in such an acceptance we shall find ourselves better able to surmount the cultural (and linguistic) hurdles. The great thing is to perceive, understand and work away from the obstacles caused by indifference.

As a study for the international negotiator, cultural influences possess an importance stretching beyond the effect of subjective bargaining. The cultural attitude of foreigners to formal contract must be understood within the matrix of each transaction. Here again, it is the difference between us and them that should be valued. An American, for example, conceives a written contract as an expression of the bargain;

but if the dealings are reduced to black and white, as often they are, he has no hesitation in making a special plea for modification when he finds it inconvenient to carry out his obligations. His sense of equity promotes a ready plea that 'I did not fully understand what I was getting into'. And no matter how naive he sounds, he expects — and frequently receives — some adjustment. The Slavic temperament runs otherwise. Hard bargaining aside, once a Russian comes to the table and signs his commitments he will be *morally* tied to them. And there is little or no probability that would advance a plea for a special consideration on the basis that *he* did not understand the undertaking. To admit this would be an admission of gross incompetence in conducting the affairs of whatever state agency was in his charge.

In other countries, the striking of hands to seal the agreement carries a solemn undertaking that will be taken solemnly, as amongst Germans. Yet the striking of hands, as amongst Italians, should not be relied upon as an absolute come-hell-or-high-water promise. Here too we may encounter the plea of 'You didn't understand what I meant you to understand', and, if the plea for modification or total exculpation is rejected, can Italians be adept at finding ways and means to delay, defer and deter the ultimate execution on their part of what was intended by both sides to be a waterproof contract.

The foregoing notes are not an indictment of contractual irresponsibility; they simply serve to warn the reader of the facts of cultural life. Certainly, contracts are entitled to performance; with equal certainty, subsequent situations might arise absolving either side from performance. But the negotiator must know early in the game how his foreign adversary's background will act upon him.

With particular regard to contracts, the foreign adversary will reflect his cultural predispositions. First, as to what Anglo-Saxons sometimes allude to as the sanctity of contract, it may be said that the *legal* implications are separated in foreign minds from the personal ethic. The preceding comments dealt with the *coming to contract* as it may be variously viewed abroad. Here we find the *fact of contract* as a bundle of precise rights and duties stated by a legal instrument treated as apart from the personal obligation. It is the personal engagement which takes precedence, strange as it seems; the legal instrument is a memorial. There is a practical reason for its comparative inferiority, namely: in foreign markets the individual is more conspicuous, more intimately known to his fellow traders, and therefore more exposed to criticism. It is one thing to receive, follow and defend a technical right — but it is altogether something else to break one's word. The latter is the act that destroys reputation and credit. The former is merely a course taken on the advice of some lawyer. The result is that business men who pride themselves on their standing in the business community, which is smaller abroad than at home, would have to consider very carefully any inclination to walk away from his hard-won reputation.

Secondly, Anglo-Saxons are sometimes oblivious of their hypertechnical reliance upon precision, and at the very same time they ignore the social sanction compelling fidelity to the oral contract. They are unaware of the cultural background, for instance, of a Romanian wine exporter who has to work his way into the good graces of his government in order to obtain the basic licenses, permits and trading approvals. They are unacquainted with the constant stream of inspections and checks upon his activities to which he is subjected. They take no account that his private and public presence is regarded as a mirror, however small, of the state. And they cannot appreciate how this cultural force becomes an omnipotent control on what he says, particularly what he says during a foreign negotiation. He is very much under the police power of his state's supervision, and were he to be caught breaking a commitment with a foreigner, the complaint lodged against him would not be dismissed lightly. Both his personal ethic and the cultural standard enforced by the state would act to keep his verbal undertaking valid, enforcible and operative.

To the same effect are the manufacturers, mechandisers and distributors of other small communities abroad. In their negotiations, allowing for their attempts to rely upon their version of *caveat emptor*, they know full well that they stand in the public eye. Once more, with reference to the vintners, everyone who has to negotiate transactions with French, Italian or Greek vineyards must recognize the singular zeal exercised not only by their respective governments, but also by their community associations, in aid of contractual answerability even when the agreement is oral. And this grave attention to oral commitments reaches into such of them as are not witnessed. The Germans, despite their pedantic particularity, hold to private agreements made 'under four eyes', without benefit of legal documentation.

Whatever has been said in the foregoing paragraphs in relation to written or oral contracts must be taken subject to the plain exception rising from outrageous deception, wilful and wanton insincerity, and a deliberate determination to flout the moral as well as the legal precepts within a given foreign community. Abroad as at home, negotiations are at the mercy of those who are practised frauds. This being so, it is imperative for the negotiator to steep himself in the cultural climate of the country to which he will be going to do business. He will have at the least some criterion by which he can screen out palpable imposters. Unfortunately, again abroad as at home, it is the sophisticated masters of deceit who do the greatest damage. At home, the minute we hear someone's 'May God strike me dead', uttered as proof of honesty, we suspect him. Not so in Italy, where persons of probity may call upon the Deity to act as their witness; it is done often, with feeling, but not necessarily with duplicity. It takes a deep knowledge of the foreign culture to enable the negotiator to discriminate between what rings true and is true on the one hand, and what rings true but is not on the other.

Incidentally, this shadowy zone of constant doubt as to what may or may not be believed was once illuminated by a very quaint convention. The English trader was held in such high esteem for his probity, that it was acceptable for a German doing a deal with a Frenchman while both were in Spain to exchange their contract assurances by giving each other 'the word of an Englishman'.

The convention is no longer taken as a talisman for explicit trust. The legality of contract overrides, in most business done abroad, the former faith exchanged between parties. Nevertheless, where the foreign side protests 'My work is as good as my faith', and prefers a hand-striking cachet of approval, it can be difficult for the negotiator to reject it. Of course, he ought not to permit himself to be gulled and lulled by the protestations of good faith. His responsibility to his company takes priority over catch-as-catch-can bargains. Nevertheless, he can try a middle way. There is no harm in suggesting that the personal faith of the foreign negotiator is not in question, but for the sake of form and company procedure it might be wise to reduce the 'good faith' understanding to a validly executed contract. In this way he avoids giving offense while protecting his company against any damage rising from what may euphemistically be called a subsequent tension of opposing interests.

Examining both the cultural and legal aspects of the foreign transaction can be more useful when we accept their integration. That is to say, it would be difficult and time consuming to separate them qualitatively. So much of culture enters into the spirit of the contract and the intentions of the foreign side that by the time the legalites come to the surface, the negotiator's prospect of doing business could be whittled away in the process of acting out the role of a lawyer. The best to be hoped for as a solution to his negotiation problem is the attainment of a relationship in principle, leaving to one side the knotty issues that might be resolved only by bearded jurisprudential experts. Anyhow, the market pressures on time and advantage are strong; they militate against missing the boat. And if the negotiator has been able to judge the credibility and character of his foreign adversary, he will be able to infer with fair certainty just how trustworthy his opponent's word is, how he will regard the written contract, and what he will do under the pretence of strict legal construction to evade its obligations.

So, in the end, culture works both invisibly and on the surface to influence the substance of the negotiation and the performability of the eventual contract; and, further it dictates, for all practical purposes, what the negotiator should anticipate when the parties later dispute the clear contract provisos.

It may be even argued that culture's importance is mainly irrelevant because the negotiator's main focus is on hard and fast business provisos, to which culture is peripheral, especially in routine sale and purchase agreements. Nothing can be further from the truth. Culture is not peripheral; it is the core of commercial reality. As an example, one of the most revealing reports linking large business transactions to corruption, bribery and a score of other criminal offenses in the oil industry has established beyond reasonable doubt that the cultural predispositions of those who exacted bribes were not residual remnants of ancient customs but, rather, active cultural influences on current practices that were systematically constructed to embrace the appearance of legality. In other words, the character of the men followed step by step the precepts and paths that had been trodden by their commercial forefathers without interruption. The difference lay in the acceptance of a contorted ethic as a mandate for common usage.

This meant, as the reports now widespread show, that the demands for bribes were not isolated nor confined to single odd instances. In truth, the bribe-takers were organized efficiently from top to bottom. Whether we speak of those in one foreign country or another, the patterns exhibited the same marks of cultural indifference to probity known in the past. And contrary to the popular view that the bribes were furtively proffered, furtively received, and furtively distributed, the public proof is that the bribes were actually dressed up in open memoranda, given the form of mutual obligations assumed by the participants, and implemented by all the legal rituals, accounting methods, and regulating supervision accorded to straightforward business transactions. Not only was this bribery widespread, detailed and in derogation of honest business it was defended by the plea that honest business was impossible, and that as a matter of business survival, the oil companies had to meet and pay the bribes demanded. In the following treatment of the place of foreign law in an international negotiation, we shall comment further on the relation between culture and legality, and add a note on what was done in Italy in order to put a good face on the oil industry's corrupt practice.

As was earlier stated, the negotiator need not be a missionary for morality, but he must be careful to know, to value and to watch out for the operative influence of a particular foreign culture as it affects good business practice. His surveillance of his foreign adversary should not be constricted by academic axioms or classroom psychology (although they can do no harm). He should know with whom he is dealing, from a standpoint of personality; he should know from where he comes, from a standpoint of cultural susceptibility; he should know what he represents, from a standpoint of legal dependability. Dealing with a foreign negotiator from any of the Western democratic countries is a different matter from negotiation with an Eastern Bloc adversary. This is so, not because the former are more or less friendly than the latter, although this is no small thing; but because their cultural backgrounds are enormously dissimilar, their cultural philosophies are at opposite ends of the scale, and because their negotiating objectives are entirely at odds with each other in terms of time. For example, western negotiators accept the existence of unlikeness, but work around to individual approaches. Eastern Bloc negotiators do not; they never relax their personal diffidence. Western negotiators are free in their style and speech; Eastern Bloc negotiators are not. Western negotiators respect their duty to their employers, yet retain discretionary authority. Eastern Bloc negotiators not only respect but are the emissaries of their state agencies, and have no personal discretion with which to modify, alter, vary, or break off a negotiation without the authorization of their department superior.

The reason for the distinction between both classes lies in their cultures. Westerners have the elastic adjustability that we expect in democracies. Eastern Bloc negotiators are tied to a cultural philosophy of self-abnegation, social sacrifice in the interest of the state, and to an economic dogma that is built on quota allocations that must be supplied to the letter, number and specification.

Some may argue that one-shot business trips abroad require little or no deference to culture because they are self-executing. This is not so. For example, one may just as well urge that irrevocable back-to-back letters of credit are money in the bank; but they are not, as anyone who has had payment on them stopped by court order knows. Furthermore, the single venture may spin off more cash flow, more profit, more repeat orders, more credit than a long-planned negotiation to establish multiple franchise outlets abroad.

Safety is important. For the negotiator it includes two elements: precaution and caution. Precaution covers the background, and that necessitates a knowledge of the foreign culture. Caution concerns the actual course of bargaining, and here again foreign coefficients of culture come into play. The personality, the physical attitudes, the entire range of behavioural indices are the crystallization of culture; and the negotiator would be unwise to slough off his supervision of the negotiation at any point short of completion.

Safety is essential to the art of negotiation, because negotiation is impossible to control unless one knows everything, or as much as one can put together, about the foreign adversary and his culture. This is not fanciful. After all, a careful driver is one who checks his vehicle before he operates it. Tyres, fuel, oil, brakes, ignition, battery and water must be right — or the car simply will not function properly no matter how skilful a driver he is. On the road or in heavy city traffic he must drive defensively to avoid the other fellow's blunders, recklessness, or sheer stupidity. Why not draw a parallel to international negotiation?

For example, returning to our earlier comment on the differences between East Bloc and Western negotiators. It would be foolish, if not criminal to try to deal with a Slavic negotiator on the basis of his individual congeniality. He is bound to avoid anything smacking of the cult of personality. For him, personality and individual preference is counterculture, reprehensible and dangerous. Indeed it is so dangerous that if he is caught out in the act of fostering friendship during a negotiation he may be reported, placed under surveillance and then subjected to official criticism which may cost him his job, or more.

This does not mean that such friendships may not be made, but if they are they are peril points. The official view of the Russians is that the state's interests preclude any personal contacts. Personal contacts are equated to personal susceptibility; and such susceptibility would place the state's security and advantage at risk. Should Ivan shut his eye to a favourable bargaining ploy, he would be placed on report and watched like a hawk. The Slavic logic runs so: friendship leads to favours; if not, why the friendship? If the friendship is personal, the state must suffer. Better that Ivan be removed and disciplined. Never mind that the still-born friendship was concerned with a comparison of Moussourgski and Mozart, or a contest between vodka and Kentucky mule, or laying odds on the outcome of the Olympic basketball games. From the cookbook formula, the Russians eschew personal friendships, and the westerners should guide themselves accordingly. Why kill a good contract for the sake of being declared persona non grata, and having the company's prospects die on the vine?

However, the negotiator must be left to his own devices in special situations. There are, here and there, exceptional instances of friendship between Russian and non-Russian negotiators — but just here and there. Arnold Hammer was such an exception, and he died an exceedingly wealthy capitalist, after an exceedingly long and productive business career with the Russians. But that is another story. For the negotiator going to Russia, he should take notice of everything and conduct his business Russian style, impersonally. Common sense might even induce him to submerge his personality in a trade commmission venture conducted under the aegis of his government. But if he thinks that he can conclude a deal on his own, the best advice is to respect the Russian cultural signs, symbols, philosophy, and negotiating protocol. If he does not, then his effort, time, and travel costs will be wasted. More impressively, if he does not keep himself to himself, so to speak, then he will find it impossible to get more than a cold shoulder; and his expectations of visa-renewal will be thwarted. If the venture at the outset really was worth putting together, why not nurse it along from the outset.

The Foreigner as an individual

It is commonly assumed that all human beings are alike because they function physically alike. Granting the physical functions, it is true, nevertheless, that the ways in which they direct their social interaction vary in accordance with their environment, their history, their tradition, their experience, their communication vehicles and the condition of their ethnicity.

There is a great deal of theory about interpersonal relations. The psychological factors have come in for very careful clinical analysis and interpretation of stimuli/response studies. For the negotiator, as valuable as these academic aids might be, it is more urgent for him to know that his Muslim colleague would be put off by pork, no matter how hospitably offered.

Similarly, his English adversary does not like to do business over a weekend; he will not find his French adversary in Paris during August; his Belgian adversary wants to see a 'girlie' show before talking contract. His Spanish adversary's best moods come into sight after a late supper. A Turkish adversary's sense of time is far different from the Western one in respect of appointments made. This does not leave the negotiator under the duress of local idiosyncracies and foibles. He is free to adjust himself to them — and he should, for he is the one going abroad to attract the foreigner. So he must set out to draw him close, not to repel him. There is a more important reason why the negotiator in fairness to himself ought to take a patient pause in being careful about foreign differences. Whatever he was able to do within the domestic market was done because he literally had a quick study available to him of familiar stereotypes. If in Yorkshire, he knew the general trim of the Yorkshireman. As an American, if in Georgia could accommodate himself to the swing of Atlanta or the leisure of Savannah. But, for example, what does he know of Caracas that will enable him to approach his adversary there?

All this has a direct bearing on the matter toward which we are pointing: the art of negotiation itself. Those abilities to convince in the domestic market rest on a knowledge of the mental and emotional responses that may be safely anticipated at home. The persuasive skill has effect solely because of this knowledge. Removing the negotiator from the domestic market places him in the midst of people whose ambitions, hopes, dreams, motivations, restraints and impulses are at variance with his own. He must cater to what he sees abroad, and he must reduce what he observes to tactics and techniques that are especially relevant to the time and place of his foreign business. By chance he may find himself successful in using and profiting from a home-country technique, but more frequently he must scout out the differences abroad and adapt his style to them.

As an example, within his own country, the United States or the United Kingdom, he might persuade his adversary by an appeal to his personal ambition, or to his egoism, or to his capacity to satisfy increasing markets. But in Russia, as is well-known, none of these appeals would make a dent in his

Russian adversary's resistance. First his personal ambition is circumscribed by his rank and file in the Soviet industrial economy. Secondly, as we said earlier, egoism is anathema to the state dogma of 'all for the state'. Thirdly, the negotiator's proposal to increase productivity would fall on deaf ears tuned to a planned economy within each sector and subsector of a design for production, distribution and consumption rigidly tied to an immutable date-line, five years hence, or however it may be extended. Ivan's personality, even were he able to raise his sights to a higher horizon, compels him to lie down and wait for the impulse to dissolve itself in personal security. He is a negotiator with a quota to be met through negotiation. That sums up his function. If he were a plant director, the quota, no more, no less, would be his target. For, obviously, a quota deficiency would result in criticism, removal and loss of perquisites, if not of party membership — a quota overshot would draw him commendation, and, upon its heels, an upward revision of what would be requred of him. Quotas suit the state; they suit Ivan. They make no waves, excite no envy, and induce no subsequent shortfall. So long as his niche in the Soviet scheme of industrial operation is filled to the letter, he is secure. It should be kept in mind that to the Russian mind and within the Russian vocabulary 'adventurer' is a pejorative, especially when applied to Westerners.

What the negotiator must do in order to make use of his tactics and techniques is to get a firm comprehension of the human being who is facing him across the foreign bargaining table. He must filter out the personality from what is said and how it is defined by the interpreter. He must screen into his reflect-register what each foreign gesture is, and what it supplies as a clue to the personality of his adversary. Tics, twitches, gestures, gesticulations at home may be read one way; abroad they have altogether different implications. The negotiator who rates himself as a fair amateur psychologist will find the foreign adversary up to a new bag of tricks.

Remembering that his job abroad opens on a hostile, perhaps xenophobic, note the negotiator ought to know precisely how he will tackle the problem of dissolving that xenophobia, producing a neutrality, creating a channel of communication, promoting a sufficient attention span, and then converting the foreign adversary's refusals into acquiescence. These phases are all conditions reprequisite to ultimate agreement and profitable contract.

Undoubtedly, the negotiator will consult handy do-it-yourself texts on behavioural psychology; and he can learn a good deal from them, some of it will surface to advantage. But his best persuasions will emerge from his appreciation of the fact that foreigners are people, different people — entitled to as much careful regard as he would devote to analyzing the statistical records of his favourite football player. Persuasion depends on 'connections' between the negotiator's approaches and the personality of the foreign negotiator (save in the Eastern Bloc countries). How can connections be made unless there is a sound sense of what is acceptable, what is unacceptable, what will induce, and what will repel? Tactics that are standard with the domestic market will have little or no impact elsewhere where the psychological makeup of the adversary does not include the same conditioning processes experienced by the negotiator.

Technique will be impressive only if it sets off the negotiator to advantage. If he makes egregious errors, and shows himself ignorant of local peculiarities, he will be treated accordingly. Finesse costs nothing but painstaking study and attention; and this means that the negotiator must not only be at the right time and place for business, but he must do the right thing, hear the right way, and speak the right way so that the message he means to convey will be heard and received in the right way.

Sometimes, negotiators abroad are ensnared by their 'acceptability' dilemma. Somewhat like American presidential candidates, their idea of achieving a 'connection' with their audience of Indians is to put on a war bonnet dragged out of some theatrical warehouse. The negotiator's war bonnet may be a fez, or a beret, or whatever headgear is pertinent to the locale; but it does not impress the other side. Either it exposes his contempt for their gullibility, or it holds him up as a clown. Dress, manner, voice, tone, tactics and technique are part of the negotiator's perceptible responses to whom he meets abroad. People do not appreciate condescension, either at home or anywhere else. Negotiators who come on strong, go out fast. The need to deal with people as people, rather than as social units must be stressed because it is critical to the negotiator's ability to convince his foreign adversary. While addressing him by whatever local honorific is applicable, he ought not to lose sight of the fact that his goal is contract, and so is that of his foreign adversary. That each may endeavour by different ways to reach the goal does not warrant the negotiator in pressing when he should suggest, when in fact he should suggest only what his foreign adversary can take in easily, without resistance. The middle way, ancient as it is, may be the only way to treat foreigners as people; and if it is, the negotiator should do so.

There should be no mistaken idea that our view of treating people as people carries with it the assumption that all foreigners are substantially alike, or that we are to overlook either their social distinctions or their personal peculiarities. What is meant simply says that the negotiator should regard his foreign adversary's basic responsiveness to human needs and demands, taken within the framework of his origins and personality. In Italy, the negotiator's sounding of the current scene cannot overlook the aura of the people's discontent recently visible in kidnappings of important industrial and commercial management leaders. How far that discontent colours the Italian adversary is a fair question. It might be answered in part by the overall corruptibility noted in the foregoing comments on the Italian oil scandals. Substitute for physical violence a propensity to violate the law and we have a partial answer to the Italian adversary's susceptibilities. By asking for a bribe to be paid him in return for selling out his company, or, if he is a public official, his people, he simply becomes a representative of generic violence. That he might have higher conceptions of his duty, that he might be disposed to uphold his moral obligations, thereby distinguishing him from the stereotype image of ready violence cannot be denied. But the negotiator cannot pass by the prevalent patterns in coming to an opinion on how best to deal with the Italian facing him across the table.

What has been said of the Italian temperament may offend those Italians whose rectitude and personal probity cannot be doubted. Nevertheless, it would be naive for the negotiator to assume that his transaction in Rome moves along on objective lines, unimpended by the possibility that through some subtle intimations from his opponent the granting of an ordinary concession can be jeopardized, or delayed if not refused, without an under the table *quid pro quo.* What applies to the Italians, has a like applicability abroad wherever the ethical standards have been compromised by the native social derangement. In extenuation for the Italian kidnappings it is artfully argued that they are merely reprisals for social injustice typified by capital's abuse of its prerogatives, and management's suppression of liberty through a perversion of the law — once again, as proven and admitted in the oil situation. This presents us with the classic query as to which came first, the chicken or the egg. But the negotiator is not in Rome to solve a philosophical or social conundrum. He is there to reach contract — and only to do just that. The fine reasoning is of less importance than the plain facts, namely: (a) corruption and corruptibility exist; (b) Italians throughout commerce and industry are aware of corruption, condone it to a large extent, and participate in it in proportion to their personal reactions to the amount of 'inducement', the safety with which it may be procured and concealed, and the freedom from subsequent detection and prosecution that they may count on. This boils down, so far as the negotiator is concerned, to a warning of the odds that somewhere on the negotiating road he will be posed with the problem of bribery, 'graft', 'grease', 'cabbage', outright extortion and all of the disagreeable collateral features of corruption. They may be disguised by euphemisms. Premiums, commissions, prizes, percentages, participations, shares, overrides, and compensation are conventional terms that assume unconventional connotations very readily. For the negotiator — before he goes to Rome — the need to know how to deal with the people there is not hypothetical; and he should not believe that he can 'play it by ear'. Once on the spot, literally and figuratively, he is faced with both his own morality and that of the Italian adversary. In addition, he must see to the position and interests of his company. How he will find his way out of the maze of moral issues depends on how well oriented he becomes to ethical priorities, as they affect himself, and his Italian adversary. With respect to ethical priorities here and elsewhere, the following anecdote may be in point as an amusing example of conflict of moral interest.

An Italian middle-man, engaged in 'assisting' foreigners to

elude strict prohibitions applicable to their negotiations, decided to increase his income by joining hands with another 'middle-man'. Together, they thrived. It occurred to them that they could multiply their income by demanding bribes from both sides to an international deal; and if one side refused, the other side surely would be compelled to submit. This agreed, it was left to one of the partners to open this new avenue of profit. He did, with such skill and poise in 'Making an offer than you can't refuse', that both sides of the foreign transaction promply paid him the required sum. He found himself in front of an imponderable question which, as he put it, was 'Should I tell my partner?'

His reasoning, a little tortured, went along these lines: 'Extortion is illegal; bribes are illegal. So the payments I collected are illegal. Since they are illegal, I owe nothing to my partner, legally. On the other hand, he *is* my partner. Still, before he became my partner he knew that I was doing something illegal and that he too would. So he should have known, since both of us were going to act criminally, that there is no honor among thieves. However, it may be safer, instead of share and share alike being disregarded, to give him a smaller part and conceal the rest.' At this point, so the anecdote goes, the partner came in, shot the moralist, took all the money and departed saying 'You can't trust anybody these days'.

In the light of what goes on everywhere in America, England, France, South America, Africa and points all about the compass, old-fashioned morality has been watered down to the question of what one can get away with. How far should the negotiator go with the tide? What is the border line between practical business efficiency in 'expediting' someone's official acts by a pair of tickets to the theatre, and doing something during the foreign negotiation that smacks of insidious corruption? The negotiator must be careful in previewing this question, for it searches out his capacity for erroneous moral judgment.

For example, suppose the negotiator takes it as a fact that all the world is a cauldron of evil, and with this in mind he goes abroad to do his company business. Arriving at Oslo, he meets Olaf and says 'Let's understand each other. How much do I have to pay to close the contract and get the next flight back to Oklahoma?'. Suppose that Olaf is as pure as the driven snow, shocked by the query, and repulses the overture. He takes his leave; four hours later he returns, having convinced himself that, after all *he* was not required to do anything patently illegal or irregular. Contracts are concluded. The negotiator waves farewell, climbs aboard the Concorde and says to himself, 'Everybody has a little larceny in his heart' while reading the thank-you note from Olaf, who is eternally grateful for the gift of a blanket woven by the Lallapoosa Indians back in Indian Reservation, Oklahoma.

Others take the position that international negotiators, by definition, are bound to take the world as they find it abroad. They must negotiate within an ambience of frailty and foibles that, however distinct from those at home, are no less natural to man's imperfections. Therefore, the negotiatior ought not to make moral mountains out of minor peccadilloes. The case has merit on both sides. For practical reasons, all that the negotiator can do is to steer clear of difficulty and danger as much as possible. Temptation and its consequences abroad are pitfalls not because they pose novel ethical problems but because the problems are decked out in deceptive, unfamiliar wrappings.

Basic principles, however tedious, are the cornerstones of any foreign negotiation. In dealing with the foreign adversary, the negotiator should be informed as to the 'W' trinity: *who* is the foreign adversary?; *where* does he come from?; *what* does he represent? The anwers to these questions provide the foundation for everything that the negotiator must encompass in his tactics and strategy. Knowing the answers with reasonable certainty, he will be able to determine just what he can say, how he can say it, and the effect it will produce. That, in a nutshell, is what international negotiation needs as a baseline for style, flair and psychological techniques. Without such a certainty, the negotiator will be adrift and incapable of intelligent control over the progress and outcome of his transaction abroad.

In considering people, we must also account for policy. Agreed, policy is expressed through the executive or legislative branches of government. But the formation of policy commences in the sense of the community. Government declares policy; the people give it substance. And within the

Western democracies policy corresponds, sooner or later, to what the people require. *Vox populi* is not an idle phrase. For the negotiator this means that he must take note of the relation between his business dealings and the community sentiment. If he fails to do so, the foreign community's resentment will be a barrier to success. This resentment rises because its well-being, its policy — however muted — stands at risk.

To take a simple example, one that occurs abroad as industrial development into green-belt countryside. A domestic company intends to assemble acreage in Besancon in order to put up a French watch factory. Community sentiment is not consulted. News of the negotiations leaks out to the local press. The policy of industrialization by the domestic company is opposed by the residents. Representations are made at Paris and plans to block the enterprise take shape. Then something new is injected into the conflict. The worker's and their union representatives at LIP, the well-known long established French watch factory, learn that its financial condition is desperate; that bankruptcy is imminent, and that employment will be phased out. They too have a sense of policy. For them, the plan to construct a new company, adequately financed, employing local labour is manna from heaven. And with them are the peripheral interests such as shopkeepers, whose vision of the LIP bankruptcy and the resulting local depression is quite different from that of the residents who desire to preserve their homes, grounds and estate against further industrialization. Local controversy bubbles and boils until the common policy is settled satisfactorily. Perhaps the residents will succeed. More likely the economic benefits will attract majority support from the workers and shopkeepers. And the hitherto inchoate economic policy will find controlling expression through political organs. Politicians need votes; and they know on which side their political bread is buttered. Whichever side comes through, the importance of policy should be plain to the negotiator. Going abroad, perhaps on a first visit as a precursor to his transaction, he would be prudent to explore local policy, local sentiment, local community feeling. If his instructions are to steam-roller over local resentment, he must see how strong his adversary is and what can be done by him in mustering the necessary political and legal forces that will make the transaction practicable. For unless the agreement can be given teeth, all of the foreign negotiations will not be worth the paper they are written on.

Examples from every kind of international business can be found for the asking. The question of the Arab boycott of companies dealing with Israel is hung on points of policy. Not only government policy or factional policy, but community policy must be consulted. Popular sentiment is a fact of the Arabian success in interdicting foreign traders from doing business with Israel. Negotiators must respect its impact whether or not they share that sentiment; and domestic companies seeking market opportunities with the Arab bloc must consider how to placate Arab community policy; they have no alternative if they find Arab business vital to their survival.

For the negotiator, it should now be easy to fit into a whole the several preceding discussions on the relevance of internationality to the business for which he will be going abroad. Culture, law, politics and people are the constituents of his industrial or commercial expectations. All of them entail a careful appreciation, and with it a suitable preparation.

The preparations required must be made with reference to the particular foreign market and the particular foreign transaction and, so far as possible, the particular foreign adversary to whom he will address himself. Furthermore, remembering that outside of the domestic market there are innumerable parallel, contradictory and confusing forces that play on the prospects of his bargaining conferences, the negotiator must reckon on spending as much time on his preparations as the importance of the foreign business warrants. Time is on his side only up to the moment of his departure from home. After that moment, everything he does or plans to do is subject to hourly pressure. If he misses out on a closing argument, the transactional opportunity may be lost forever.

There can be no doubt that more foreign business is lost through careless and mistaken preparations. Even more fail to mature because of inadequate attention. In the main, of course, in foreign negotiation the objectives have been selected by the domestic company rather than the negotiator, and with them the cut-off point for the bargaining. Nevertheless, most negotiators are allowed reasonable scope for their functions, and have more than an educated guess to guide them to the background information compiled by their company. Indeed, were they sent blindfolded or blinkered, there would be little or nothing they could do abroad other than act as mere couriers. The failures in foreign negotiation occur less because the objectives are ill-chosen by the company than by the strategic and tactical measures employed by the negotiators. Needless to say, negotiators are prone to explain the failures by assigning them to causes outside themselves. This is human, forgivable — and unnecessary; unless they have been sent out on impossible missions, they are chargeable with the failures and the blame is theirs alone.

Chapter 3

An insight into foreign law

The dangers of illicit dealings; the limitations of home government protection; the role of a company lawyer; the importance of local knowledge.

Even before he goes abroad, the negotiator may expect that the foreign legal climate will vary from his own as much as the cultural climate varies. The points of legal difference will not only impinge upon the formation of his eventual transaction but also on the terms and conditions by which it will be governed and their expression in written instruments.

At the start, the 'connections' earlier suggested may be deemed permissible at home yet restricted or totally proscribed elsewhere. A case in point is the conduct of business in the Italian oil industry, where the Italians have accepted special preferences as part of their negotiating framework. They are reported to have agreed with a group of oil companies on a percentage, 5 per cent, to be paid for advantages granted to the group. The percentage was fixed by determination the money value of the accruals. To bring this scheme into effect, a network embracing retailers, wholesalers, oil storage depots, lawyers, politicians, — and even the entire Italian cabinet — was worked into the plan. The objective of the plan plainly was to allow the oil companies exceptional profits by promoting concessions, creating artificial concessions, and enacting special-situation legislation, including tax reliefs. The network assumed the face of legality until uncovered. British oil interests were compelled into the operation, they say, simply in order to do business and survive. Italian investigators of crime take the position that both the Italians who demanded and received the 'inducements' by which the scheme was effected and the oil companies who paid the percentage, running into millions of Italian lira, violated the moral and legal restraints against such conduct.

What approach should the negotiator foresee when, at home, he seeks to compete against keen competition that is prepared to adopt illegal and unethical measures? As to the unethical conduct, that is a matter of conscience upon which this discussion need not, indeed cannot, dwell beyond taking note of its importance. But the legal perplexities must be prefigured or else the negotiator will mistake his course, subject himself to legal penalties and his company to disastrous consequences. If he deliberately ignores the law's impositions and says 'The law is an ass', as have others here and abroad, he may find to his dismay that the ass has a powerful kick.

Both American and English negotiators may be assumed to respect the constraints of foreign law, less because they agree with the manner of its impingement on their transactions than because they believe it senseless to court time-wasting trouble in defying it. Some exceptions exist, as they do in all things. Occasionally, as in the Italian matter, or the Poulson one in England, or the ITT involvement in Chile, the prospective prize is so large that the English or American companies believe the game is worth the candle. And for them it is, until they are caught.

In a brief conspectus, when we address ourselves to the impact of foreign law we are touching the practical not the philosophical considerations. Whether or not the foreign law embodies the rights of man is not tabled for discussion. Whether it assists or deters the transaction because it regulates exportation, importation, strategic materials, free trade, tax imports, currency controls, labour and working conditions, social security, severance pay, health and medical services, manufacturers' warranties, retail merchandising outlets, union/management agreements, two-tier directorates, nationalization, patents, copyrights, commercial paper, industrial processes, raw material and refineries, inland freight, forwarding and transport, tie-in sales, and, at the end, the formalities for reaching and executing contractual documents — foreign law is all pervasive and is to be observed, even if it does not accord with the law at home. That there are many loopholes, evasions, and willing foreign collaborators abetting a flouting of what must be done is too plain to be argued. But when the game is up and friendships are betrayed, or errors discovered, or ordinary outrage at unfair practices rouses competitors to complaint and prosecution, then the candle is seen as a very flickering and illusory light, blown out by the least breeze of enquiry.

So as to understand the character of foreign law with regard to internationality, we must accept the limitations of extra-territoriality. That is to say, the power of our own government can reach a protective arm over us — and shield us when we are beyond the borders of our country, but only up to a point is this true. When our presence on foreign soil is taken as a license for wrongdoing under foreign law, intervention on our behalf by our government is available in very particular instances and not as a general rule — and even within the particular instances protective intervention is not available to every trading Tom, Dick and Harry. Business men of no commercial importance or social consequence who are caught dead to rights, as the expression goes, while out of the country, cannot entertain even a hope of help.

Furthermore, the negotiator going abroad may be affected by domestic law even to the point of limiting the activities open to him. If he passes outside those limitations, it is domestic law that will penalize him. Such limitations, as are placed on entering foreign politics, exporting strategic minerals, fomenting or forwarding transactions contrary to 'anti-dumping' legislation, not to mention the requirements for reporting taxable income derived from international business, must be foreseen and seriously weighed. Agreed that the domestic government's barriers to negotiations in one country may be down with regard to another; but that only increases the need for learning them. If our government is more concerned with what we do in China than in Zaire, then we should be thoughtful in each case — and have in view the consequences following our negotiation presence at either place.

Real life situations are not those depicted in fiction. The negotiator does not arrive in an impenetrable cloak of mystery, unnoticed and unattended. He does not escape detection while he makes his rounds. His movements are subject to reports, rumours and enquiry. In comparatively democratic countries he will enjoy a looser kind of movement; in those having a totalitarian administration he will have virtually no freedom to rove. In a foreign country he will be subject to its strict legal supervision, and this is just as true in countries that are common market members. While the members' subjects and citizens have been the beneficiaries of ambulatory flexibility, their actual trading scope is fixed by EEC, EFTA or such other controls as bind the members into a common association. Dealing with an economic community member implies the need for knowing the legal effect of its regulations, tribunal decisions, enactments and practices. The body of law evolving from EEC itself is different in many ways from the laws of the member countries. And the laws of the member countries reflect the impact of community law; in their search for concordance, foreign countries constantly seek enabling legislation that changes the former face of law within their territorial frontiers. Foreign law is now in a state of continuing modification. The negotiator going to a particular foreign site ought not to rely on what he gleaned from a kerbstone opinion years ago. In fact, even if he has had personal experience in that place, he would be very well advised to check the current trend of its law.

How does internationality affect the negotiation? There is a scale of a kind that commences with the negotiator. At one end of the scale, his arrival at a given city constitutes a submission to the prevalent foreign law. As an individual, he becomes personally answerable for his presence, movements and conduct — all of which must be seen in submission to the law of the place. Moving along the scale, the negotiator as representative of his home company figuratively takes his company with him. Literally, his company is exposed to liability arising from the negotiator's conduct if in contravention of foreign law.

Ignorance of foreign law, even less than ignorance of domestic law, is not an acceptable excuse for infraction, offense, misconduct or criminal activity. While spitting on the pavement may be a minor infraction at one place, it attracts a graver reaction elsewhere. So it is also when dealing in contraband. What constitutes contraband depends again on the law of the place, and not on the negotiator's plea of innocence of the law. Again, personal liability, and that of the home company, for personal injuries resulting from transgressions of foreign law may be incurred merely from conversation. For example, if the negotiator is too enthusiastic in decrying the quality of his foreign competitor's merchandise while extolling his own, he may find himself embroiled in litigation on charges of defamation that could never have been laid against him in his own country. Similarly, if his persuasions overstep his discretion and he adversely criticizes the political system abroad, or is even *thought* to be doing so, there is a more than fifty-fifty chance that he will have to make some kind of retraction or face the consequences; and in certain countries consequences can range from reproof, expulsion and fine to immediate physical attack, followed by arrest, confinement or worse. One need only read the news reports to see that incaution by business men abroad is now an invitation to incarceration. As an example, nothing could be more judicious for the negotiator than the Japanese, 'See no evil. Hear no evil. Do no evil.'

In essence, the negotiator must see the law as central, not peripheral, to what his business may accomplish. In every foreign country, and perhaps at home as well, lawyers have been the subject of cynical humour. The figure of plaintiff at the horns of the cow, defendant at the tail — and the lawyers at the udder — is all too familiar, and unjust. Arguments and experiences to the contrary are numerous. Nevertheless, assuming that they hold some merit, it is still incumbent on the negotiator to orient himself properly by taking adequate competent opinion as to the legal circumstance of his foreign transaction — before he goes away from home. Who else but a lawyer has the training, the time, the interest, the expertise, and the negotiator's interest at heart? And if the company lawyer needs a wider ambit of legal reference, he can always arrange to have the opinion of a foreign colleague made available for the negotiator as a further safeguard.

The negotiator can be armed with all the legal advice in the world, but that will not suffice if he acts in derogation of it. Imprudent speech, conduct that flaunts the foreign customs, meddling in local affairs, pronouncing gratuitous and unwelcome judgments on local government, assisting a local business man in some nefarious dealings, consorting with persons under suspicion of political insurrection, failing to comply with routine registration requirements, carrying firearms without license, violating currency controls, even refusing (albeit with pretext of right) to pay hotel bills, or any of innumerable trivial failures to do in Rome what the Romans do, can be a roadblock in the path of his company's objectives, while engaging the foreign police in expediting his arrest and expulsion.

On the other hand, assuming that he has taken his foreign mission seriously, acquainted himself sufficiently with the legal dimensions of the area, and holds himself with appropriate urbanity and dignity, he reduces the likelihood of offending anyone; and, simultaneously, he improves them in favour of completing his transaction and returning with a good contract. Parenthetically, and fairly, it should be said that even negotiators who are paragons of decorous virtue can be, and are, caught up in foreign intrigue, chance affray, chicanery, and false imprisonment. All the more cause to be careful. Competition abroad is cut throat. Rivals stop at nothing they can get away with; fair play is notable for its absence. They employ a repertoire of subtle and crude devices to debar anyone who threatens their share of the foreign market. The negotiator cannot lend himself to their machinations without endangering his company's interests as well as his own. Disgruntled rivals are potential informers. And the information they divulge under the cover of anonymity may be wholly false, tinged with just enough truth to cause the negotiator some very unpleasant hours of explanation in some country where the art of explanation is practised unsuccessfully. Disappointment and rancour can stir up all kinds of trouble. 'Well-intentioned intermediaries' may try anything from commercial espionage to outright blackmail, given the opportunity for intimate acquaintance. Vexed officials are known to exceed their official duties when not placated by 'inducements'; and, on the other hand, if they are not given enough 'grease to make the wheels turn', their indifference to transactional necessity can be enormous — so that essential registers, stamps, approvals, and endorsements never come to view. Here again, combining law with common sense and worldliness can do no harm.

It is worth noting that many of the foreign entanglements

abroad do not proceed from deliberate dereliction. Many negotiators are too pressed for time to consider, let alone pursue, the safeguards. And the idea of consulting counsel before doing foreign business may be regarded as an admission of incapability to bring off a deal independently.

The contrary is true. Taking time to find out what law governs the foreign country respecting the major aspects of the business makes good sense. But it is also useful to know the law applicable to motor vehicle collisions, police interrogations, overcharges, false representations, shortchanging, gambling debts, and what to do when the revolution comes squarely in the middle of the negotiating conference. Trying to get a lawyer in a foreign emergency is not a piece of cake. A number of them are afraid to have any dealings with outsiders. Some of them have to hedge their political contacts and would hesitate to defend an outsider against a local government official's misconduct or indifference. The problem may rise to considerable heights when the negotiator is far from home and his consular friend is inaccessible or away, or under instructions to keep a low profile, or under house arrest.

Chapter 4

Political problems abroad

A case in point; economic influences; the importance of involving local political figures and of preliminary investigations.

Culture and law lie within the negotiator's foreign province; and with them he must account for the nature and form of foreign politics when looking at the international market. There are several ways of assessing the foreign political situation. For example, if the negotiator follows the narrow field of his transaction, let us say, in acquiring land for development on the Costa Blanca, he cannot avoid a vista offering probabilities of upheaval ensuing upon the restoration of the Spanish monarchy. Nor can he close his eyes to the need to cultivate an acquaintance both with those who are well-situated in the present government and with those who stand a chance of replacing the present government's officials. Politics for him is not an academic interest, it is vital to his hopes and prospects.

For example, the author was recently negotiating with a view toward instituting an urbanization near Denia, and as it was shortly after the death of Franco, the resurgence of liberal and anti-liberal forces became a matter for conflict in Barcelona, and of course a question had to be considered respecting the effects of the conflict on the project. The key query was pragmatic enough — if the liberalization of Spain commenced in the Catalan region, and spread southward from Barcelona to Denia, would that threaten the proprietary interests of the urbanizing shareholders? In short, how strong was the evidence of nationalisation as a political probability? The next point to be mooted was that of getting approval for the project itself. The installation of utilities, the provisions for water, the minimum requirements of plottage, the essential access roads, not to mention all of the other stages to be agreed, depended on municipal approval. The mayor of Denia was an important pivot. What would his successor be like? In fact, who would his successor be? What assistance might be granted easily to the developers of the project? What difficulties would lie in procuring architect-approval, in procuring all of the other consents by municipal authorities, national offices, and how long would it take for such approvals and consents to be issued?

The single source of information on all of the vexatious items lay buried in some bureau in Madrid. The next best course had to be followed by indirection, through taking the pulse of people on both sides of the political fence, at local and national and regional, especially regional levels.

At the time of writing Spain is in the midst of a promised constitutional reform, along lines that elsewhere would cause not the slightest stir, but, in Spain amount to post-Franco radicalization, Catalonia is turbulent. In the cities, Madrid alternates between attempts at moderation and suppression of the liberal leaders; Barcelona is the very epicentre for successive waves of civil intransigence; the Basques are indomitable, intractable and militant. And all of the forces of imminent change, in any direction, make it a Herculean task merely to coordinate the operative elements of the urbinization, those concerned with land-clearing, terracing, road-building, grading, and the furnishing of power, light and water.

To begin with, in order to organize the project on efficient lines, the steep slopes must be made accessible for labour and materials. This requires access roads. Roadbuilding and land-clearing need bulldozers and other machines. The access roads must reach into the autopista, the main highway cutting through the region. This takes money. Outside investors are reluctant to come in because of the unsettled political future. Nationalization could nullify the investors' expectations of returns. More than that, it could present a stony-faced response to the needs for speedy response to requests for permits, approvals and consents. Perhaps even more important, the urbanization, even were it to proceed apace, would reach a cul-de-sac with respect to purchasers of improved land. Who would want to live in mountain-homes that could be isolated by roving bands of government and anti-government forces? Finally, even the participating landowners are not of one mind as to political preferences.

The urbanization project, happily, is feeling its way forward, but slowly; and delay is raising the costs of capitalization day by day. This is a classic instance of the impact of politics on internationality itself, and, more closely, on a foreign negotiation that commenced with a straightforward land purchase cum development and sales programme. The expected stage by stage movement toward completion simply became derailed by political uncertainty. Even the anticipated troubles with official bodies seem minor compared with the prospect of sacrificing money, effort, time and intelligent coordination should the Spanish political atmosphere take on extremism from either doctrinaire partisans or stand-fast monarchists.

With reference to purely industrial/commercial foreign negotiations, every accustomed step must defer to the political temper of the times. It is mandatory for the negotiator who thinks in terms of erecting a warehouse on a foreign site, or looking for secondary financing within the foreign country, or opening shopping centres, or establishing a factory to see politics as an ever-present factor, and one that must be calculated as precisely as possible.

One way to give the calculations protection is to translate the enterprise into politically valuable terms. And, in turn, this links up with the local economy — not to mention the total foreign economy. The starting point for such calculation is the realization that the introduction into any foreign community of new opportunities for production or distribution produces an immediate change in its economy. The negotiating objectives should be geared to highlight the changes as beneficial, and to underplay such of them as might not at first blush appear to be so. Thus, a transaction aimed at setting up an assembly plant can be translated first into economic and then into political positivism, thereby eliminating the antagonists whose chief complaint is sounded along the lines of absentee-owners drawing off the profits at the expense of the exploited local business interest. In this way, the assembly plant transaction becomes a source of greater employment, increased social opportunity, more per capita disposable income, larger volume of retail sales; consumer investments and purchasing power will be channelled into new housing, new clothing, better food, better municipal facilities, greater technical and educational opportunity, and vastly improved cultural appreciation, as aided by theatres, cinemas, libraries, and so on.

Moving from the economic to the political themes, the negotiating techniques should stress repeatedly the responsibility of the local political figures to their constituencies. By supporting the transaction, then, the figures themselves, will acquire greater scope for their part in improving the welfare of their communities. By doing so, they will attract favourable notice for their future candidacies either as incumbents seeking to remain in office or seeking elevation. This theme can be carried forward earnestly, honestly, and in keeping with the local realities. It need hardly be said that on its own merits any programme that seeks the improvement of a community's well-being speaks for itself. But, if, in addition, the local political support is essential — and is weighed in with the economic rationale, the chance for a successful business agreement is enhanced substantially. Incidentally, the introduction of the assembly-plant, or whatever is sought by the negotiator can be presented so as to allay the fears of those who have reasonable cause for apprehension. As to those whose outcry is factitious, or fictitious, they are usually brought into line by the local political forces — aided by a helpful public relations policy, well-advertised communications with the community leaders (as by meetings, conferences and discussions on a man-to-man basis). And for those who decry the transaction because they fear, or allegedly fear, a siphoning away of the moneys rising from the enterprise, it is enough to present them with a projection of the actual economic improvement to be derived, stated by percentage, graphs, real values in terms of wherewithal, savings, and community pride. To the same effect, if the transaction is to be 'sold' to the foreign company, then the negotiator can address his efforts toward the economic and political benefits the foreign company must draw from its increased standing within the community, its influential position with trade association, and its accrued importance in union/management relations both at the site and wherever else it may be industrially or commercially involved. In the latter case, the negotiator's perception of the line running from economic to political to particular profitability should be elucidated to the point where it speaks for itself in terms of sheer logic. None of the foregoing comments makes it imperative for the negotiator to try personal intervention with the local community officials. As an outsider he should soft-pedal his role, letting his political friends act as his channel of communication, for their dignity may resent his bald intervention. Indeed, it is the best part of negotiating wisdom for him to eschew any appearance of partisan intruder. A lot of political dispute and rejection, no matter how it might be dressed up in fine appeals to mother, home and country, takes its impetus from injured political vanity.

The negotiator aware of the political nature of his business abroad, and keen on avoiding the traps and pitfalls of obvious intervention, can locate his political advocates, as well as those who might oppose his mission, by preliminary investigation into the local scene. He can compile a useful dossier on whom to cultivate, whom to sun, whom to treat at arm's-length. He can cover himself with a reserve of alternative political friends. This will educate him to the *dramatis personae* in local political circles, and in so doing will keep him on the right political side of the transaction. If the negotiator turns his head away from this suggestion and primly forswears political acquaintainces abroad before he knows what he will run into, is carrying the punctilio-of-an-honour-the-most-sensitive theme to an escruciating simplification. Every politician, for better or worse, has something to say, a stick to wield, along the line to political power; and political power, as we have seen in the previous comments on the Italian oil situation, ties into economic power, which is related to the foreign business sought by the negotiator. This does not commit him to immortality, unethical behaviour, or unforgivable intrusion into foreign politics. There is nothing wrong in knowing men in key positions. Nor is there anything wrong in asking them to do what they should do, especially something that will benefit their people. And when they improve their community and the people within it they can only better their own position. The

Italian case was an example of something entirely different. The Italian political figures, according to the reports, did not improve their community. On the contrary, they deprived their people of essential fuels in order to aid, for a scandalous bribe, the oil companies' purpose in reaping exceptional profits. Admittedly, the moral line is fine, difficult to ascertain, and sometimes invisible. But it is assumed that while the negotiator is a pragmatist, he also is as alive to his moral obligations as the next man, perhaps more so because he is on the front line of any conflict that will attract publicity.

Having laid out the political relevance of contacts with foreign office-holders, what should the negotiator do to promote them? And how should he go about it?

The answer has been hinted at in the foregoing paragraphs. He should devise a method of linking the political importance of the project to the specific foreign office holder; and with this done, he should enlist the support from the office holder in favour of the foreign transaction. The technique depends on the negotiator's style and the politician's ego. The effect of the linkage will be seen in the results. First, the negotiator will be better received when he lands at the foreign negotiating site. Second, he will have a friend at court, so to speak, who will act as a political godfather to the transaction, and third, he will be able to impress his foreign adversary with the prestige of the domestic company. After all, coming in as an outsider under the shield of a local political figure is no small feat. The kind of linkage sought here begins before the negotiator leaves his home base. He can get in touch with his company's bank manager, and through him with the foreign branch of the bank. Circular letters of introduction, accompanied by personal certifications, are customary. Even though they tend to sound negative, they are interpreted as they are meant to be. Thus 'X has had an account with us for ten years. His account has been satisfactory. He is well known to us in his capacity of director of Y company. We consider Y company a friend of our bank. We would appreciate any courtesy you may extend to X'. Nothing extravagant. No fulsome statements of personal attributes possessed by X. No confidential matter related to his transactions. And, it is important to note, nothing is indicated of the bank's position in the foreign business. Anyone reading the letter as an understatement would be correct, up to a point. If that anyone had commercial experience, he might draw his own conclusion as to the bank's expectations. In any event, when the negotiator arrives at his destination, presents his accommodating papers to the local branch manager and lets him cast his eyes over what is said while he considers what he should do, the momentary pause usually terminates with a polite 'Ah, yes. How can I help you?'. And this is the right moment for the negotiator to ask for an introduction to Foreign Politician W, subject of course to the bank manager's views of W. The rest follows as night follows day. At an informal meeting, perhaps at the bank manager's home, or office, or club, or even at the local consulate of the negotiator's country, the negotiator and W heap compliments on each other, and size each other up. A later meeting is agreed, and then the negotiator will have plenty of time to open his business to view. Naturally, he will display it in general terms, and only so much of them will be revealed as may require the furtherance of W. It is important for the negotiator to know a good deal of the personality of W; and it is extremely important for him to exude all of his charismatic effluvia. Assuming that he can charm the birds off the trees in his own backyard, he should make a determined effort to charm W. For from that moment on, assuming W has the political power associated with his office, the negotiator can get much of his useful background work done through W. Even more, he can have W take in tow such arrangements as should precede a formal conference with the foreign adversary. For example, if the foreign business looks to a triangulation involving commodities to be stored at a free port pending trans-shipment, W should be just the man to clear the way for their storage and quick release as required. So, by the time the negotiator and W visit the foreign adversary's offices, storage and trans-shipment are no longer open issues. The same theme of linkage can be developed by other approaches, either taken individually, or in conjunction with the bank sponsorship idea.

For instance, the negotiator might ask his consulate to refer him to co-patriots presently engaged in non-competitive business abroad; and then through them explore useful connections with politically helpful personalities. Or he can apply to his own member of the House of Commons, or of

Congress, for a contact with a similar deputy in the foreign country. Or he can work his contacts through the International Chamber of Commerce. Doubtless, his own trade association will have had experience within the same foreign country and will be helpful in designating an available foreign sponsor.

The negotiator must remember one rule. While on foreign soil he should make friends, never enemies. The latter can be most inconvenient, even when not actually malicious. The former can always be relied on to vouch for his character. And character reference is extremely important abroad.

Chapter 5

Preparations for going abroad

Market surveys, feasibility studies, desk research field reconaissance, physical verification, continuation reports.

The aim of foreign negotiation is to reach agreement. Agreement depends on a knowledge of the relevant facts and the ability to transmit that knowledge agreeably. When the opposing negotiators accept the premise of the promises to be exchanged, the transaction may be concluded and framed within appropriate instruments in writing.

This summary suggests more than it says. For the negotiator to know the relevant facts places him under the duty of analyzing them positively and negatively in order to set them out attractively. His ability to pass on the attractive features and touch on the drawbacks without destroying the transaction is in itself an art that does not grow on trees. It takes a great talent to persuade someone, especially in a foreign country, that a possible flaw or risk or liability does not hit at the heart of the business. There are two ways to exercise this talent. One is by a grandiose invitation to the foreigner in the form of 'Trust me, everything will be all right'. Foreigners are not fools, nor do they repose trust carelessly. They, like us, figuratively bite the coin to test its genuineness. They, like us, will say no to the invitation. The other course is to possess such an intimate and thorough knowledge of the facts as facts, and, in addition, a knowledge of the market itself, so that the facts can be taken and judged within the context of whatever movements are afoot. This is the sound way. And its course begins right at home. For the negotiator, or his company, can rely on a market survey to fix with certainty the entire market scene and the factors that will militate in favour of the transaction; and knowing these two constituents of the transaction gives the negotiator the confidence for his persuasions abroad. He can relate the disadvantages candidly, and reduce them to their reality — and in speaking of them during the bargaining sessions, he need not fear dealing with them and meeting the criticism by his adversary that such facts might attract.

What are 'facts' in one situation may not exist in another. A market condition at a given time is a fact; when the market changes, so does the character of its 'facts'. Consequently, we may agree that every transaction, despite its similarities to others, still retains a quality of uniqueness that must be sought out, certified as true, and distinguished during the transaction.

This factual search for information relates directly to the negotiator's ability to introduce proposals, reject them, modify them, and come to final agreement. Without having ascertained the facts, he is powerless to reach contract. Some facts centre on technical matters. Others are concerned with legal terms. Still others may be 'soft' facts, such as rumours touching the credit-worthiness of a proposed purchaser. All of the facts operative on the foreign market and on its representative figures are germane to the foreign negotiation, for all of them, to a great or small degree, act in some influential combination on the probabilities of (a) reaching contract, (b) contract performance, and (c) profitability.

This requires the negotiator to take pains with his factual preparations. Some information can be collected personally, as by an on-site investigation, or by a physical appraisal or by an examination of public record. There are various means by which the negotiator might educate himself in preparation for the negotiation abroad. His discretion can determine which, if any, of these means will assist him, and which will not add to his negotiation. Occasionally he will have the opportunity and the occasion to use only one means. Perhaps the cost will not be worthwhile for one piece of business, but will be fully justified by another. Business that can be acomplished solely on the basis of quotations submitted by telephone, telex, cable or mail may nevertheless require verification against hard information, such as credit reports down to the last moment of negotiation. The great thing to be kept in mind is that the negotiator in possession of the facts can acquit himself of his function successfully. Without the facts, no matter how effective a persuader he may be, he is like an elegant automobile without a motor — all outside, nothing within. And in a foreign negotiation, the negotiating motor must be powerful enough to cutrun the competition. The market makes the transaction as often as the converse is true; so the negotiator's knowledge of the market is critical to success.

How does one amass information about the foreign market? This is a logical starting point. There are many conventional pulse-takings of the market. All of them can be satisfactory some of the time and under certain conditions. Some of them are simply not available all of the time, or are dated and limited, or are useful as an index rather than a report. Others speak to trends and are merely educated guesses. But, assuming that the negotiator has them all at his finger-tips, every information source can aid him in its own context. There is no single source that precludes the use of any others. And the question of how much information should be placed in preparation takes us back to the anecdote about Lincoln. When asked 'How long a man's legs should be', he said 'long enough to reach the ground.'

The common-sense of the answer applies to negotiation, and foreign negotiation in particular. Ordinarily, management makes the decision to 'go international'; and the decision is based on whatever management has learned of the foreign market. This preempts the negotiator from doing anything further toward fact-gathering. Nevertheless, often enough, management will allow him a reasonable range of further enquiry. Indeed, in some transactions, management directs its negotiations to keep their ears to the ground and learn whatever currently might affect the decision to go abroad.

From the negotiator's standpoint, that of formulating persuasive strategy and tactics, the more information he possesses, the more effective can his persuasion be. And since the ultimate selection of his technique, flair and style for a specific negotiation abroad will be tinged by what he knows of the intellectual, and emotional, makeup of the opposing adversary, it follows that he would wish to furnish himself with every kind of information that can comprise another weapon in his armoury. Positive or negative information, certain or vague information, hard or soft information, statistics, calculations, all are grist for his negotiating approach to contract.

Thus a tip that the foreign company's president is a candidate for political office, or that the foreign company's bank accommodations are curtailed, or that the foreign government will be well (or ill) disposed toward the transaction, or that the foreign market competition is increasing, or that the foreign company's material sources are in short supply, or that its credit line is reduced, or that its directorate has been re-organized, can and often does bear upon the outcome of the foreign negotiation, and, even more relevantly, it can and does influence the form and substantive elements of the desired business.

Whether the information is raw or screened, classified or declassified, is less important than the fact that the negotiator should be made privy to it. In the context of his negotiation abroad, every datum may lead to something else to be taken into account. He himself, against his own experience as a negotiator, should be able to evaulate the information, retaining the relevant and using it as prudence indicates.

There is a loose parallel between military intelligence and commercial intelligence insofar as both are occupied with a process of discovering the nature, strength and capabilities of the opposing forces — and, equally importantly, both seek indications of the 'enemy' intentions. To this end, the means by which information is sought, gathered, collated, and assessed depend on establishing linkage with some useful agency in enemy territory.

The company's determination to do business abroad places upon its negotiator's shoulders a critical responsiblity to deal prudently not only with the intelligence concerning the other side of intended negotiation, but also with that concerning his own company. For every negotiation, at home and overseas, inevitably leads to a discovery of company information that, were it not for the negotiation, would be held in confidence.

Once a company agrees to negotiate, it may expect to be called on — to a great or small extent — to reveal facts, figures and market relationships that ordinarily would be guarded in secrecy. Thus the negotiator has to know when, how and to whom he can safely reveal his company's affairs. This is no small matter; for often a foreign company might open a negotiation for the very purpose of getting close to information not otherwise available to it. Of course, if the international business goes well, no damage is done. But if not, then the burden rests with the negotiator to minimize the potential damage of disclosure.

To summarize, in every foreign negotiation information, positive, negative, hard, soft, raw, screened, plays an integral part and can be of immense operative significance.

Market Surveys

Wherever a foreign transaction is under consideration, whether it be a proposed investment in an existing enterprise, or commencing a new venture abroad, the company should have a conspectus of the foreign market realities. And this means that an estimate of the situation abroad should be made by taking into account the company's objectives. Even if the returning report be preliminary, or tentative and dependent on further field research, the company should use it as a base for determining the size of the market, the extent of government policy, the nature of the competition, the pricing structure, the limitations on the expected opportunities, the existence or non-existence of adequate facilities, the availability of man-power, the current practices in references to terms of payment, the accessibility of enforcement mechanisms, the probabilities of tax exemptions, the location of physical plant, proximity to raw materials, reliability of suppliers and assemblers, inland freight accommodations, warehousing, user requirements in respect of acceptable standards, norms for quality control, merchandising, distribution at local or other points of sale, specifications of any kind that are or may be germane to the business sought to be done.

It is the responsibility of the company to set its own survey requirements and then issue instructions to the market experts, toward having them find out precisely what is required. No academic exercises and essays are sufficient when particulars and specifications are needed. The requirements, often spoken of as parameters, should be laid out by the company — although there is reasonable ground for selecting them in conjunction with the survey people's advice. The motivation for a market survey, apart from its sheer utility, is to encourage the company to go forward in a favourable situation, hold back in an unfavourable one, or — occasionally — to spend some money and effort in creating a favourable one. Research-and-reportage by qualified agencies is a useful assurance that the proposals abroad are not wishful, speculative or beyond the realm of performability. Market survey instructions can be reposed in confidence where necessary. Certainly the company would not wish to broadcast its intentions, and thus be placed in a position of bidding against itself.

The survey can be as general or as specific as the company cares to make it. In the end, after it is complete, the negotiator ought to be given a view of it, and invited to read it for the purposes of his negotiation. It can do no harm for him to be told that he is free to add his comment; occasionally, if his remarks be seen for what they are worth, some useful suggestions can be drawn from his evaluation. Perhaps some element useful to the negotiation will have been omitted, or an error taken into the report by inadvertance. In any case, the confidentiality of the report should be stressed, and the negotiator bound to respect it —until released from the need to do so.

Occasionally, a preliminary survey of the market will serve usefully at less cost to the company, which, if the report be favourable, can then provide for a comprehensive supplement to be supplied. Such a preliminary report can supply the company with a broad definition of the foreign market; or, as required, it can concentrate on a special topics, as for example, the ownership and control of the foreign company, or its foreign corporate image, or its estimated share of the market, or its creditworthiness.

On the part of the negotiators, it is no admission of inadequacy for him to examine the information made available in the market survey. Rather it demonstrates a lively and intelligent alertness to whatever information has or may have an effectual bearing on his function abroad. Indeed, where his company opens its information sources on the foreign market, this might be seen by him as a vote of confidence in his discretion as well as in his ability to deal with the actual foreign situation. And if the negotiator, in consequence of his inspection of the report, concludes that some of the data reflected therein is insufficiently noted, or in error, or subject to correction because of market changes, then it can but redound to the benefit of his company.

In any event, the market survey intelligence is important both for what it suggests and for its omissions. It acts as a basis for the formation of the company's negotiating objectives, and furnishes a lead to the future prospects of the foreign venture. By taking into account all of the queries reflected in the parameters upon which it reports, it satisfies the company that its decision to go international is well-founded, or, alternatively, impractical. In either instance it is useful.

Feasibility studies

Two questions must be answered in relation to management's decision to look abroad. The first enquiry has been discussed under market surveys. It supplies the foundation for a decision in favour of the venture because the market abroad is right. And 'rightness' means that within the scope of time and circumstance the market is capable of meeting the desiderata of the company. Such market capability affects the negotiating objectives and, by derivation, the negotiating strategy, tactics and technique. Of course, if the market capability is negative, then the company will sit tight and postpone an extension of its operations until a more favourable report of the market can be made. The second question turns on the suitability of the company itself. It asks whether its organisation, capital structure, available financing, experience, equipment and management to this question presents a mirror of the corporate existence, and in sum amounts to a candid diagnosis of its strengths and weaknesses. It functions as a thorough 'physical' examination of a boxer before a fight, appraising him of what he must know to defend himself, and, simultaneously, of the limits of his efforts, within which he must guide himself in order to prevent excessive strain, damage or injury.

The determination of feasibility takes account of the company's economy through a factual assessment of its anatomy analyzing its trial balance sheets, profit and loss, cash flow, credit/debit position, capital holdings, operational capital, accessible risk capital, accounts receivable, write-offs, tax liability exposure, upset value. It includes an estimate based on physical plant, machinery, tools, equipment, with adequate allowance for obsolescence. Stock-piling, inventory, goods in transit are also accounted for, as are distributive facilities, merchandising, sales methods, and projections for a specific period of time. Whatever can or may affect its ability to take, undertake, and execute its foreign business successfully must be appraised realistically. Whatever conduces toward the foreign transaction should be weighed, and with it everything that can militate against going abroad.

A feasibility study conceivably need not limit its purpose to a reflection of the company as it stands now; it can and often should balance its report with a view of the company's position as it would stand after the entry into the foreign market. The effect of such an entry, and the localization of the effect, if possible, might be within the task of the feasibility study. Here, as in the case of market surveys, the guidelines for the report are pre-set by the company in most cases. Some companies entrust the feasibility study to an agency free of any hint of restriction. They leave it with the agency to canvass the situation on its own. Of course, it is described with enough particularity so that the study can tie in the company to the venture. A report that is objective still needs to relate its findings to the purpose for which it is being made—otherwise its findings do not signifiy. Thus, a feasibility report can only be useful when it effectively demonstrates that the company is capable of supporting a particular project. A purely general statement that it is healthy does not meet the purpose. 'Healthy' or 'capable' — without connection to the company's foreign venture — cannot define the company's true potentiality in terms that fairly set out its capabilities, unless those capabilities are measured by the intended foreign demands.

In feasibility studies, it is essential to pay close attention to the distinctions between a corporate entity and an un-incoporated company. The reason for doing so lies in the distinctions between the two forms of doing business. An unincorporated business, solely owned, or a co-partnership, acts mainly through its owners. And the owners possess an intimate bond to the business, far closer than that presented by a company chairman or a president of an incorporated business. The death of an owner immediately affects for better or worse, the entire life of his business; and in a co-partnership the business itself is seriously altered by a successor; whether because of his wishes or his capabilities or his personality, death or serious illness, or dissolution of a co-partnership so that a retiring partner is replaced — can radically influence negatively whatever future was foreseen for the enterprise. A corporation existing in perpetuity, managed by a board of directors elected by the share-hlders, is far less seriously exposed to adverse consequences if one of its officers resigns, becomes gravely ill, or dies. Thus, when a feasibility report is made it should evaluate the leadership of the unincorporated company with great care — for a change in leadership may seriously hamstring the future operations of the company to a degree far beyond that effected in a corporation on the loss of its officer.

In another sense, the capital of an unincorporated company and its control by individual owners should be understood as integral to the feasibility report. For personal credit is far more closely associated to an individual owner than to a corporate share-holder or to a corporate officer. Again, the character of the individual owner or of the co-partners has a more a direct impact on the company than, for instance, does the character of a managing director. Whether we speak of a sole or co-partnership ownership, the personality quantum is something to be weighed carefully by those preparing the feasibility study.

Specifically, the death, long illness, withdrawal, resignation or misconduct of a sole owner or a co-partner always shakes the company more than a similar event would a corporation. The cash available for new risks, or to meet outside demands for liquidity of assets reaches more closely into the unincorporated company, and touches the ability of its owners or owners to rise to the occasion. So the creditworthiness of the owner, or owners, is something to be taken into close study. For, assuming that the foreign venture is agreed and entered into, its subsequent demands for fresh capital, or even for continuing support may be prejudiced if the co-partnership or individual owner no longer are the same as when the negotiation abroad commenced.

This takes us back to the need for the feasibility report's inclusion of 'possibilities' with special reference to unincorporated businesses. A condition precedent for foreign business capability must be the continuance of a foreign commitment. How can it be assured? Single transactions, 'one-shot' purchases present no complexities — although even there an alteration of unincorporated ownership can raise problems. Assurance as such may not be a function of a feasibility report, yet the indications of the need for such assurance may properly lie in its embrace. What is to be done regarding shifting capital to 'bail out' the sole owner or the co-partnership when money is needed abroad to maintain the foreign venture? The feasibility report might cover this question. It cannot content itself with merely noting the trading patterns of the company as adequate — for market changes can wreak havoc with a condition that presently is reportable as 'adequate'.

For both incorporated and unincorporated companies, the feasibility report must, first and last, state accurately and fully what the present status is, how it may be subjected to change, the market forces that must be withstood, and the alternative resources upon which the company might depend in order to perform its foreign commitments.

Obviously, a feasibility report that favors the company's capabilities to carry through a foreign project is desired; nevertheless, a true report is quintessential to the negotiating function, whether it be favourable or not.

The company might very well decide to do foreign business despite a discouraging report. Indeed, it might be compelled to do so by the very nature of its current unsuccess. And for this reason it is only sensible that the negotiator know in advance the boundaries of his strategy. Negotiating from weak positions is not unusual, and very often can be turned to advantage — so long as the negotiator knows the truth. The weak points can be dealt with appropriately and the strong ones can be capitalized. But to this end, as is plain, the negotiator must be accurately oriented to the company position. If he is not, then he may innocently overstate, understate, or misstate his proposals so that they amount either to blunders or misrepresentation.

Ideally, the negotiator should enjoy the confidence of the company and use it; an advantage in planning his strategy lies in his opportunity to examine both the market survey and the feasibility study reports together. The first points out the market prospects, and the second shows how the company can employ its facilities to exploit them. Together, they defend the negotiator by saving him from taking the company beyond its economic depth in his proposals abroad.

Once the negotiator educates himself to the actual status of the company and its resources, then he can tackle the market elements intelligently. In other words, the market survey report will express itself in terms of probabilities for profitability, trade practices, dimensions and character of the competition, share-of-the-market prospects, local government policy and regulatory practices, physical facilities, such as ports of entry, lighterage, docking, piers, receipt and storing, warehousing, inland forwarding, work forces, current trends in doing business, immediate and anticipated end-user requirements, and whatever else may be pertinent to the success of the company. Matched together with this, the feasibility report, discussed before, provides the negotiator with a perception of both sides of the ngeotiation's objectives. He can look at his company not only as his responsibility, but as it would be seen through the eyes of the opposing negotiator.

Before, during or after the negotiation — assuming it will be approved and undertaken, the negotiator can refer to any section of the market survey and feasibility reports and procure supplemental information to keep him posted on whatever changes have occurred or are occurring in the market picture, or in the makeup of the foreign company. Perhaps a personality profile brought up to date will reveal a foreign company officer substitution that will improve the venture abroad. On the other hand, it may show that the opposing negotiator's function is merely a screen for an attempt to penetrate security and procure confidential material and violate the agreement for secrecy. Without too much difficulty, the negotiator may use the feasibility and market reports as negotiating check-lists during his bargaining sessions. Thus a preconception of proper plant-siting can be verified or negated by comparing the reports with the negotiating conversations issuing from the other side. Statistics, calculations, data as such arise during the negotiation can be considered against the prior reports so that the negotiator reduces the likelihood of having to accept his adversary's statements as fact, or being misled by his inaccurate versions of the facts. Additionally, by being able to back up his own position factually, he can reduce the risk of personal controversy during the negotiation.

It is always of importance to maintain an atmosphere free of acrimony or charges of bad faith or deception during a foreign negotiation. Within one's own country a certain latitude exists for 'puffing', for badinage, even for friendly insult — not so abroad. Some foreigners take umbrage where none is given cause to arise. So the negotiator, when armed with an accurate brief of negotiating information, can set the pace and form the climate for the foreign negotiation on terms that are best for doing business, rather than for engaging in personal dispute as to what is or is not a fair statement of any given facts.

Again, it is not unknown that 'getting one's goat', or 'taking the mickey out' are virtually standard baiting devices during some negotiations abroad. Even thick-skinned and vanity-free negotiators can be drawn into losing their tempers by charges levied against them, impugning their sincerity — or worse. Here too, possession of correct information, backed up by verified agency reports, can assist the negotiator, veteran or tyro, in keeping himself on the track of the objectives — rather than flying off the handle and defeating his purposes, or being pushed into a negotiating corner by psychological pressures. Style depends on self-possession. The less susceptible a negotiator is to personal affront, the greater will be his control of the bargaining procedures abroad. Having authoritative knowledge of the market, of his adversary, and of his principal's capacity to enter the transaction, he can sit through the negotiation safe against attempt to deceive or distract him into error, if he desires to lose his appearance of nonchalance for tactical purposes, he is free to do so. But he should never be goaded into this by a challenge aimed at his veracity or by one meant to discredit him personally and cause him to suffer a loss of face. Collateral arguments, pretended offence, and numerous other forms of denigration are to be expected abroad — and to be avoided. the best shield against them is possession of the true reports on what the market looks like and to what degree the negotiator's company may capitalize on it.

Desk Research

Accepting the market survey and feasibility report as useful in all cases, and indispensable in many, nevertheless a number of companies may not have available the leisure or the money, or even the desire to underwrite full-scale investigations. In some matters, it is inappropriate to provide for market and feasibility reports because the intended foreign transaction is not important enough in terms of net returns. Still other situations are enveloped in security requirements where the leakage of information can imperil the probabilities of success. Whatever the reason, it can be accepted that the negotiator appointed to go abroad and seal a contract with a foreign company will be left to his own devices, and entrusted with the responsibility for searching out various kinds of preparatory information.

Allowing for the fact that his background will have encompassed special sources of information, there is, withal, a mass of general reference to which he can gain access without too much difficulty, without too much expense, and without too much delay. The following suggestions in themselves will help his preparations; and doubtless they will open other research avenues:

1. Daily news reports, domestic and foreign.
2. Commercial and industrial association journals.
3. Banking and business reports.
4. Special studies by government departments for commerce, trade and industry.
5. State Department papers publishing news of treaties, trade and tariff regulations.
6. Export-Import Bank bulletins and advisory services.
7. Chambers of Commerce, and Institutes active in development of foreign trade.
8. Commercial insurance company reports.
9. Business libraries, for specialized information.
10. Department of Labour bulletins, statistics.
11. Economic analysis of foreign company operations.
12. Credit reports on designated companies abroad.
13. Stock and commodity market reports and quotations.
14. Arbitration tribunals at home and abroad.
15. Library references; also works and digests, statistical reports on merchandising, secondary financing.
16. Publications of stocks, sales and earnings data.
17. Shipping advice, for arrivals and departures of cargo vessels.
18. Political analysis of foreign countries.
19. Advice from foreign agents and representatives.
20. Consular offices at home and abroad.

In addition to the foregoing, much information can be derived from making enquiries at merchant banks, mercantile houses, and, of course, lawyers and accountants ordinarily can direct the negotiator to other reliable sources of information, such as public relations agencies, patent and copyright lawyers, and standard academic treatises, such as concern, for instance, commercial paper and banking practises abroad.

Not to be overlooked, although not within the strict

classification of 'desk research', is the enormous amount of information to be gleaned from reading related to the foreign site of the negotiation. Anything from a well-written novel, a detective story, a scientific paper can produce fresh viewpoints — as well as an insight into the ethnic, and ethical, predispositions prevalent in a particular country abroad.

As an instance of researching serendipity, just before an imminent negotiation with a Russian, a certain negotiator was casually placed in possession of a rather dry history of Russia, translated ineptly into English. To amuse himself, he opened the work somewhere in the middle and whiled away an hour with it. In doing so, his attention centred on an explanation for the Slavic tendency, in general, and the Russian, in particular, to act by committee rather than by straightforward personal decision. Up to that moment, he had always assigned that trait to an inability to form a clear determination. But to his interested amazement, he discovered that the habitual resort to consultation and shucking off of responsibility, while apparently dilatory and ineffectual, actually produced practical results, of which freedom from individual liability was not the least. Small as the clue was, it enabled the negotiator to address his proposals in a manner that would not compel his Russian adversary to stick his neck out, or endanger his personal safety, or submit himself to official criticism instigated by some bureaucratic rival.

Finally, the cinema is not to be despised; although it too is not 'desk work' strictly speaking, it can enrich the negotiator's comprehension of words, phrases, gestures far beyond what his academic knowledge of the foreign country, its language or its people may possibly suggest. Obviously, such opportunities to study the 'enemy' are best met with abroad. Yet even at home, he can do nothing better than finding a foreign film and studying it.

Field Reconnaissance

As a general rule, management's consideration of a foreign business may be preceded by an on-site visit to the foreign country. The visitor chosen for the occasion may be a company officer, or the company's foreign agent, or some established representative. In some instances, the company may request a foreign official from the appropriate government bureau to inspect and report on his findings. Thus, where the company means to build a local factory, an official report can be useful as a first line of information. Further enquiries can always be launched from time to time in order to round out the picture. Entirely apart from the previous discussion of market surveys and feasibility studies, the negotiator might find it extremely useful to make his own reconnaissance of the foreign scene, and it should not be overlooked if he can get his company to consent to it.

There is nothing to equal an early autoptic inspection of a plant under construction; and to the same effect, a quiet visit to a community where casual questions can supply the means for learning something of the personality of the resident directors is invaluable. Indeed, the field reconnaissance can be made in depth so that real properties, plant structures and equipment, machines, tools, transportation, research and development units, loading devices, and any other relevant items can be examined at close range. This is of first importance when the foreign negotiation will concern inventories of goods, wares and merchandise. Markings, descriptions, gradings, packing and packaging, and present condition or deterioration can be noted timely and reported to the company. On-the-spot exploratory conversations with the foreign company officers, directors and agents can be rewarding to a marked degree. Seeing them on their home ground — in advance of the negotiation — will accustom the negotiator to their style of speech, movement and behaviour. And, of course, with especial regard to the negotiation itself, he ought to be able to express his preferences concerning the place where it is to be held, the kind of staff that will be at his disposal, the availability of translators, the accessibility of office machines — and, very importantly, the kind of communicating facilities that will be at his command while abroad. At home, before the negotiation, the negotiator's primary interest lies, naturally, in the topics to be discussed, and the strategic and tactical methods he will rely on. But, when he goes over for a reconnaissance he will be able to see for himself how important the secondary items related to the negotiation become. Any of them can spell the margin of difference between an agreeable or awkward negotiation, or even the difference between a successful or unsuccessful one.

An auxiliary opportunity connected with a field reconnaissance might be considered in this way. When going abroad one never knows, even when one is a tourist, what circumstances may arise wherein a dentist, a physician, an accountant, a lawyer, an insurance representative will be required. For the negotiator, dealing in a foreign country which is or might be subject to upset of one kind or another, an early trip abroad should include scouting out the possibility of engaging professional help for himself. He ought to be able to supply himself with a number of options and alternatives, so that if his original choice as a lawyer cannot be met because of, as an instance, probable conflict of interests, then another might be managed. Even the matter of hotel accommodations, local taxi service, connections to other cities, airline reservations and the like should not be overlooked. In large cities they still can offer obstacles; in small towns and outlying foreign regions they can constitute a substantial problem; and it's best to know beforehand — rather than be embarrassed on the spot.

Something ought to be said about foreign official holidays. As a rule they are observed. The degree and kind of observance conceivably may affect the consummation of a negotiation. The negotiator can do no harm by determining from first hand sight of the foreign place just what is or may be the result of a local holiday celebration. Are the banks shut? Are offices open? A loss of a day may not matter; on the other hand it can frustrate all of the previously prepared work. It is the plain responsibility of the negotiator to foresee small as well as large events touching on his business transactions abroad. One thing more can be said. On his trip abroad, he should apply himself as closely as possible to a personal surveillance of everything in view, so that he can fit its relevance together with that of his pending negotiation.

Physical verification

As a matter of common sense, physical on-site verification of the material elements of the negotiation goes hand in hand with an early reconnaissance. The time for such a verification varies with the purpose to be satisfied. If the business abroad concerns a single sale of rawstuffs, a survey by a competent surveyor can be made at any designated point. Thus, a spot-check during loading, or a more thorough one on board, or a final certification at the port of entry can be agreed. The object of physical verification is to ensure that what is to be delivered matches, qualitatively and quantitatively the particulars of the contract. Provisos adequate to this purpose should be the subject of immediate concern to the negotiator. It saves him from the egregious error and embarrassment of buying a pig in the poke for his company. First of all, it places the opposing party on notice that thorough performance will be demanded and enforced. Secondly, it removes the temptation, to which the other side might be subject, to palm off substitutes or give inadequate measure, or deliver below-standard materials. And, so far as plant, machinery or other equipment may have been represented as meeting a standard, apart from variations from the representations, it is up to the negotiator to arrange for a sufficient verification that will reach into the origins of and title to the plant and other items. An exterior view, for instance of oil tanks, is not a warranty of their contents. An eye inspection of plant does not reveal its legal status as free and clear of liens, mortgages and other encumbrances. A bank statement or credit report, alone, cannot open up the true financial condition of the foreign company or its guarantors. In short there can be no reliance on any presumption of regularity or continuance. The duty rests on the negotiator to provide his principal with specific verification; and physical verification is indispensable. This is especially pertinent to agreements calling for installment deliveries and payments.

In the first instance, that of deliveries, vigilance is essential to verification. The negotiation must see to it that every delivery measures up to contract terms; and the measuring process must be agreed. Again, if he is to commit his company to accepting commercial paper, shipping documents, warehouse receipts, or even cash — it is up to him to supply the means for verifying the genuineness of the payments to be received and accepted. Commercial paper must conform to acceptibility as laid on by local banking and trade practices; shipping documents, particularly important in letter-of-credit transactions, should be free of doubt as to 'on board', 'since shipped' or any other condition. Warehouse receipt cannot be presumed valid until they are physically traced back to their source. So, in a recent case where they were given and received as security for financial advances, and the receipt was not cross-checked, it developed that the subject of the warehousing, oil held in storage tanks, had been siphoned off and spirited away — and the warehouse receipts had become part of a chain of fraud and deception ... all of which might have been forestalled by a timely physical verification, renewed during the life of the transaction. In the instance of the warehouse receipts, the storage tanks were almost literally sucked dry, and along with them so were the brokerage house that dealt in them, the banks that put out loans in reliance on them, and the ultimate purchasers of the receipts. Continual surveillance, early reconnaissance, and dependable physical verification are actualities to be set in motion by the negotiator of every foreign transaction. His failure or omission to do so, whether from sheer neglect or a cavalier disregard of human nature, can only place his company at risk. It is foolhardy to disregard common sense; and it is virtually criminal to leave his company exposed and without recourse.

Some negotiators on thier journeys abroad are taken in by 'hospitality', by grand manners, by one device or another meant to close their eyes to the larceny buried in the hearts of men. 'We can trust each other' is a phrase loaded with dynamite; and it is only the careless, or egoistic, negotiator whose ears will not prick up to the danger implicit in such a declaration when made by a new opposing colleague, on foreign soil, with whom one has diametrically opposing interests. Indeed, the phrase is dangerous enough when made with those one knows intimately. But with them, there is a small margin of safety, since they can be investigated readily enough.

Continuation reports

With greater or lesser effect, and despite the increase of explicit and implied warranties abroad by statutory enactments and competitive necessity, *caveat emptor* remains a reality. The negotiator for foreign business acquisitions, commodity purchases and, indeed, for the purposes of any transaction must combine his agressive interest in closing the deal with an awareness of the snags, pitfalls and entrapments rising from a careless assumption that the other side's representations are to be taken as given.

A continuation report is most of all, an extended affirmation of the foreign company's capability to meet its stated obligations. The affirmation varies with the circumstances; and its form will follow the subject matter bargained for. Thus, where the contract entails a payment in cash the negotiator must be certain that the foreign buyer actually possesses funds at all times up to completion. If there is a requirement for quota deliveries against installment payments, the negotiator must determine that the installments will be met on the due date — or, if any of them cannot be assured, it will not be because of the foreign purchaser's financial instability or lack of immediate funds. With regard to consignment sales, via a local representative of the foreign buyer, the negotiator ought to provide for the safe receipt, storage and transfer of the subject of the consignment. Adequate terms should be supported by whatever physical facilities are needed abroad to cover the consignment. The function of the report is to police the negotiation and to give its ultimate bargain substance. It acts to eliminate surprising changes. So, as it works its effects on real property purchases, the continuation report will assure the domestic company that its purchase will not be subject to last-minute encumbrances or conveyances to other purchasers by the foreign company, or those acting in the foreign company's chain of title. The negotiator cannot assume anything, least of all that what was valid and in existence on Monday will still be so on Friday. Whether it concerned the transferability of a copyright or the assignment by the foreign company of its right, title and interest in certain proceeds of a liquidation, the principal point to be kept in sight is the continued existence of the subject of the bargain and the surrounding circumstances.

It has been mentioned in the earlier pages of this work that due care and caution are needed in taking the foreign negotiation towards a contract. It may now be said further that care and caution should be strengthened by continuation reports recording whatever changes, if any, may adversely affect the domestic company. Take an example, as in an 'all-requirements' contract. Suppose that between the opening of the negotiation and its conclusion, the foreign manufacturer disposes of his plant, tools, machines and other equipment, and that he does so with an honest purpose and intends to replace them. Where does that leave the negotiator? He has no assurance that, at the time for delivery of the 'requirements' by the foreign company to the domestic company, the replacements will have been made; or, if made, that they will be good, sufficient and operable. How does he find out the relevant facts? First, his continuation report reflects the event of disposal. Secondly, it notes the replacement, if one has been made; or, if none has been made, then it calls the negotiator's attention to that fact. Assuming genuine good faith on the part of the foreign company, the negotiator may suspend the negotiation, or alter the frame of reference so that, for a temporary period agreeable to both sides the domestic company is left free to supply its needs by resorting to some other manufacturer — long enough to permit the domestic company to maintain its standard operations without interruption or loss of materials.

Another benefit of a continuation report is that it gives the negotiator an insight to other market changes affecting the transaction. A recent example was the decision of the Dominican Republic to warehouse all of its sugar rather than supply it at the market price which it regarded as unaaceptably low. Suppose the foreign company was a wholesaler of Dominican sugar and was negotiating with the domestic company for its sale. By having a continuation report running during the transaction, the domestic company's negotiator could do two things: (a) he would be able to notify his company immediately of the decision by the Dominican government, and (b) he could continue the negotiation on an if, as and when basis. This would leave the domestic company free to search for other sources while maintaining contact with the wholesaler. In fact, any commodity transaction is extremely sensitive to market fluctuations, and since those abroad are greatly influenced by national, as opposed to economic, movements, it would be improvident for the negotiator to lose touch with the policy of the Dominican government as it acts on his proposed contract.

In the main continuation reports ensure regularity by virtue of their enduring surveillance, keeping the foreign side 'honest' by preventing them from going to contract on conditions they know are materially different from those bargained for. If this reads as a condemnation of foreign traders, the interpretation applies with equal force to domestic ones. Certainly, the foreign companies are capable of maintaining a watch on whatever is central, or even incidental to their negotiating interests.

The volatile international gold market exemplifies a further need for continuation reports. Prices go up and down within minutes, and it would be absolutely ill-advised to negotiate without reference to the latest information. This may seem fundamental yet losses are made continually by lack of such information. These losses are occasionally the result of bad judgment, radical market factors, unexpected interventions, and the like. But basically they are attributable to lack of contact with the real situation in any given market.

What continuation reports provide in their function may be seen as information on one hand, and a sense of value on the other. For it is value, in the long run, that forms the final conclusion of the advantage or disadvantage of the foreign offer. What was said about gold, obviously applies to shares of stock. The continuation report keeps the negotiator intelligently current with (a) the foreign company in true position and (b) with the overall market movements relevant to the negotiation's subject matter. Unquestionably, the negotiator's preparations should foresee the need for and provide for the receipt of a continuation report. Should he omit this common-sense precaution because of egotism or simple oversight, he is in danger of taking his company into a losing contract. The fact that remedies may be available does not help his case. Litigation is long, costly and debilitating, and arbitration is not much better. It is obviously wiser to do the right thing and do it properly, remembering that 'an ounce of prevention is worth a pound of cure'. It may be admitted that well-experienced negotiators are egotistical, as they must be to assert their client's position persuasively. Indeed, very often it *is* sheer egotism — when they are seized of the divine afflatus — that closes their eyes to a simple safety-hatch through which they can lead their companies to secure contractual positions. The American oil fraud, mentioned in Chapter 2, is a classic example of the need for every measure that will provide safety. Whether it is by physical verification or continuation reports, the principle is the same.

The mechanics of continuation reports

The first step is to make the tentative negotiations subject to the incoming intelligence by agreement with the other side. There is nothing to be lost by letting the foreign company know that the eventual contract will rest on the true final state of facts. Second, engage whatever reportage is essential. This can be very straightforward, as in the selection of physical verification of physical facts from professional sources. In every branch of commerce, industry and finance there can be found trustworthy and able reporters, whatever their designation may be. Third, make it a point of caution to provide for the free dissemination of information from the reporter to the negotiator at the foreign conference. If the line of communication is blocked or inadequate, the information will come in too late, or in too incoherently to serve his purpose. Fourth, agree with the foreign adversary on the acceptance by him of the report. This will put both sides in parity as to their negotiating good faith; and the negotiator will not feel that he is engaged in some act of furtive espionage. Nor will the foreign adversary have any cause to take offense.

Chapter 6

Communication

Language; translation; interpretation; semantics; nuances; verbalization; non-verbalization; physical signs; signals; attitudes; silence; immobility; functional psychology; group and behavioural patterns

Language

International markets require, as do those at home, a satisfactory exchange of terms leading to a business relationship. The relationship itself is part of the concept of a social structure tying together the wishes of the parties. In order to build the structure of transactional ties, they must be clarified with requisite precision. The precision needed to express the tie, or contractual term, is defined by the kind of relationship sought. And this relationship tends to dictate the language employed by the parties. Language acts as the medium for transferring from one party to another certain images. The images actually are ideas that, in any negotiation, assume final form because of the modifications worked by one party on another during their bargaining. In the domestic market, the initiation, modification and completion of these ideas flow along common cultural and linguistic channels. Even so, the ultimate coincidence of the parties is not instantaneously perceived. It emerges from their reciprocal understanding, at last, after the images have been subjected to intellectual and emotional consideration. To stir both sense and sensibility, each party directs linguistic stimuli toward the other's susceptibilities, seeking to implant favourable reception, extirpate unfavourable reaction and germinate assent. The instrument to this end is a selective technique which, whether or not it succeeds, is what we define as persuasion. Reversing the order of what has been said, it would be plain that persuasion would be positive and effectual in those instances where the images were found attractive by the parties whose consent was required. And, of course, the images would appear so only where the language was in fact adequate and suited to the common cultural concepts shared; mutuality, then is the keynote for contact.

Abroad, the passage of images is impeded because of the absence of a common culture and a common language. The negotiator must overcome this by his comprehension of (a) the kind of images the foreign adversary can grasp, (b) the kind of words and phrases that will connote these images, and (c) the cultural forms that will receive and accept the images. In short, the negotiator's way toward a useful transaction, wherever he may find himself in the international market, has to overcome the differences governing his and his adversary's imagery. It makes the process of doing foreign business more complex, obviously, and such complexity must be respected.

For the negotiator to tackle the complexity, he must begin at the point where he admits that what he wants to say, may need to be phrased in accordance with the kind of foreign culture to which he addresses his business and the kind of language that is employed within the culture. A simple example taken from home market selling vocabulary will make the psychological point clear. Merchandising a product in three packages respectively marked 'Small', 'Medium' and 'Large' is less likely to lead to sales than if the packages were sold as 'Large', 'Extra-large' and 'Giant-size', where the customer is concerned with product quantification. On the other hand, where price is the cogent factor, marking them as 'Home-economy size', 'Lasting-supply', 'All-purpose' adds consumer appeal and elicits a more positive response.

In a foreign market it cannot be assumed that the domestic market appellations will be satisfactory. For instance, it is unlikely that the local consumer habits are the same, or that the home equipment and storage facilities are as commodious for storage of the 'Giant-size items', or that they would not spoil over an extended period of exposure, or evaporate, or lose their operative qualities. So the negotiator, if he were on a foreign selling mission would have to discover the local cultural patterns and apply them to his product prior to selecting the right language for transfering the image of his product into an image that would be acceptable within the local practise of cooking, cleaning or whatever was relevant to his home-use product.

Total coincidence of image between the negotiator and his foreign adversary hangs on other cultural appreciations. The negotiator sees himself as a person. The foreign adversary looks at him and sees a foreign individual. And this at once alerts the adversary's innate fear of intruders *qua* intruders. But the latent xenophobia does something more; it ignites a pervasive distrust that can be overcome only if, as and when the negotiator can summon up the right images, and select the right words — foreign words — that will dispel the distrust. This comes down to the relative skill of the negotiator in instilling his adversary with amicability; and, in turn, the negotiator can summon up the right images, and select the right words — foreign words — that will dispel the distrust. This comes down to the relative skill of the negotiator in instilling his adversary with amicability; and, in turn, the negotiator must establish his credibility as an individual and as a unit of the society he represents. In other words, his product or purpose, or both, are intertwined with his personal presence.

To follow this thought through, we say that the negotiator's ability to set up a working relationship with his foreign adversary rises solely from his persuasiveness, and that the end of the persuasion, if the foreign adversary is to be convinced, should be the acceptance of the negotiator's imagery as it describes who he is, what he means to do, how he means to do it, and how believable he is in his own right and as an agent for the domestic company.

Logically, it ought to be as easy as rolling off a log for the negotiator to do the needful. However, there is a wide gulf between seeing what is required and doing it. Within the context of this discussion, we must recognise that we are not seen as we see ourselves. Therefore, abroad, we must translate our personalities so that they will be seen within the ambit of the foreign adversary's favourable experience. Our love of ourselves, to bluntly state the case, prevents us from doing so. Sometimes, we go to the other extreme, and try to obliterate our personal characteristics instead of thrusting them forward. A middle course of imagery is the solution; and, to be sure, as we said at the outset, language is our vehicle to this end. If we use it properly, we can create the images we need, and in doing so literally replace those of the foreign adversary so that his transactional hopes, expectations, desires and requirements are those we wish him to have. When this is done, we may say that we have given proof positive of our credibility and that of our purpose abroad.

Finally, the negotiator must always exercise due care that the foreign language selected by him will correctly depict his objectives, and simultaneously, that he will always be presented through it as he intends to appear — for if he does not persist in maintaining the requisite imagery, he will lose credibility for himself and his transaction.

Vocabulary expands our range of imagery. So do physical movements, gestures, facial grimaces, attitudes and postures voluntarily exhibited. Perhaps more so, do those involuntary evidences of our reactions, such as flushing, blushing, perspiring, gasping and blanching. Any experienced negotiator knows this. Some seek to offset the uncontrollable evidence of their inner selves by exerting conscious effort. 'Poker face', 'Stone-face', 'Bead-eye' physiognomies occasionally succeed in partially doing so. Another way of disguising our responses, is by deliberate dissimulation, exaggerated changes of pace, and so on. But whether such deceptions work their tactical ends abroad as they do at home is debatable. After all, the cultural differences lead to different inferences being drawn from what we may say or do thus misleading our foreign adversaries. The same is true of language. For example, at home we might register enthusiasm by saying 'Wonderful idea'. In England, equal support for a proposal might be found in 'I see no objection at the present time'. The cultural time and place, the cultural use of language, the linguistic mechanics of communication all form an inextricable whole of negotiating imagery. Indeed, even mere vocalization, wordless in itself, can suffice in conveying something of value by way of an image. Germans use 'Ach' in a multitude of ways to express sympathetic response. We describe a jet-plane's swift rise by 'whoosh'. Going beyond this, shoulder-shrugging, world-wide, speaks of doubt, indecision, indifference, unconcern, stoicism in the face of inevitable events or even of simple ignorance. Thigh-slapping needs no verbalization or even vocalization to demonstrate approval. On the other hand, depending where we find ourselves abroad, a smile does not necessarily infer approval, friendliness, humourous assent, or whatever we at home habitually associate to it. A grunt, howl, embrace, back-turning or eyebrow lifting must be taken within the cultural mould. Heterogeneity complicates the progress toward exact comprehension by either side in a foreign negotiation.

Our easy domestic imagery, our ability to push our ideas into ready linguistic forms, our capacity for 'getting a rise' out of our regular companions or strangers within the domestic market, all become paralyzed, lamed or contorted when we find ourselves abroad. The negotiator must see, accept and defer to the necessity of absolutely correct image-communication. For this he should think of his international mission as more than a flying visit entailing no more than is required to take a proposed written contract for signature. He will find his business more certain and the proposed relationship more agreeable if he proceeds to the foreign country with a wholesome respect for its cultural moulds and linguistic forms. And in place of limping through the negotiations, creating even more hostility than he might have anticipated, beating the drum for disagreement, he will meet courtesy, indulgent curiosity, and a tolerant consideration of whatever he may have to suggest on behalf of his domestic company.

Foreign imagery is pithy, suggestive and usefully affords an insight into the speaker's background and attitude. The Italian 'potatoes don't grow overnight' airs an acquaintance with the need for patient, cautious supervision of a business dealing coupled with an anticipation of the possible difficulties that may intervene between the commencement and the conclusion. The French 'all cats look grey at night' is a recognition, with typical Gallic humour, that the intended transaction holds no distinctive advantages — but merely serves the necessities of the occasion. An American seeking to establish a service agency might enthusiastically say that it 'is capable of anything'. The same phrase to an Englishman could be understood as attributing a capacity for committing murder. And the English objection 'You are putting the cart before the horse', has a homely practical ring; but the same thought in the American 'You're jumping the gun', takes another tinge. The former implies a premature procedure or sequence of ideas; the latter carries the same connotation to which is added the idea of unfair overreaching.

The examples of Slavic imagery are equally down to earth. whether the negotiator will be charged with overstatement, as in the phrase 'You are beating an empty teapot', or with proposing a useless arrangement, as in 'taking samovars to Tula', the folk-experience directs the phrase. International negotiation needs more than literal accuracy to convey the concept. It needs local imagery. And this need can be met by using a competent interpreter in preference to an academically qualified translator. Translators undoubtedly are first rate for exact wording; interpreters are better instruments for sending and receiving the mood, nuances and intentions of the parties. They render the feelings more fully and more subtly. And it is important, indeed critical, to foreign business that a sympathetic response is nurtured. Without comprehending the character and background and emotional content of the foreign adversary, the negotiator's persuasions would have to be directed almost solely to the technicalities of the subject matter, and thereby would lose much of the force required to convince. In order to draw emotional responses, the negotiator should be able to stimulate them; and acceptable imagery is a direct road to this end, to be travelled in company with an interpreter who knows the relevant foreign language expertly, and who is capable of employing it imaginatively, easily and suitably.

The burden of providing a suitable vehicle for communicating the terms of a foreign negotiation lies with the negotiator not only because it is necessary for him to make his way in the foreign milieu, but because he must accept the need for establishing and maintaining a harmonious relationship throughout his dealings abroad; to do this he must see to it that a flow of trade terms goes smoothly — and the best method of doing this is by selecting and using a responsive interpreter. The time to select such a person is not when the negotiator appears at the foreign company's offices. He ought not to wait until he meets his adversary before determining on an interpreter. The first moments of encounter count for a great deal; and if they are neglected, considerable leverage can be lost. The better practice is to search out the interpreter beforehand. Depending on the nature of the transaction, the place abroad where it will be discussed, the time available for doing business there, and the local circumstances to be envisaged, the negotiator's enquiry can be begun from his home base. There are usually available any number of directories listing expert interpreters available abroad. Reference to local consulates will be helpful in locating a reliable interpreter. And, in foreign countries, as at home, there are teachers at universities, polytechnic institutes, and language schools who would be happy to hireout their services. Early correspondence with them can ensure that they will be on hand when the negotiator arrives. In the interim, it can do no harm for him to remember that he will also require faithful renditions of such documents, minutes, notes, descriptive materials, collateral memoranda, technical literature and government papers as are related to his business. It is as much his responsibility to provide for his accurate written communications as for his oral ones. Perhaps it may be said that it is even more important for him to be able to take in and reply to the letter and sense of written materials than to verbal exchanges. In any case, his rule for safety should make him aware of adequate preparation in all sectors of communication as vital to his success abroad. If the foregoing comments about available interpreters abroad are followed, communicators (interpreters and translators) can be engaged timely. A wider choice of them may be had by taking recommendations from local chambers of commerce, banks, or local (non-competitive) commercial and financial houses. The main thing for the negotiator to remember is that his communicating instruments, human and mechanical, must suit his requirements.

Translation

There are various kinds of translation that domestic businesses use to advantage in sending and receiving terms, bids, and offers. Straight translations are wholly literal, providing word for word accuracy in rendering the foreign tongue into English and vice versa. Thus, in routine matters, such as transactions for nuts and bolts, machine tools engineered to micrometic precision, and personal services within particular fields, the function of translation is clear and supplied without difficulty.

On the other hand, paraphrasing translations run beyond the absolutely literal and give the explicit sense of the transactional exchanges, affording parallel understanding by each side of what the other intends to be understood.

Translations are helpful because they are close to the text of verbiage, and therefore the opportunity for error is reduced. This is particularly true for technical descriptions of trade terms. Again, translations are impressed with what the communicator desires, rather than with any optional inference to be drawn by the recipient of the message. The disadvantages, as well as the advantages, are apparent.

In face to face negotiations, translations ignore the personal quantum; this is not so by mere chance but by deliberate choice. As a result translators do not possess the wider ranges of bi-lingual expression because they are not invested with the liberty to go beyond the textual matter, or to add to it or to subtract from it, or, most importantly, to impart to it the collateral signals that could convey other than what the words themselves say.

Derivatively, translations, then, are not fully flexible for the purposes of persuasion; most certainly, they cannot encompass the full implications of idioms, slang, colloquial usages or personal peculiarities. For example, the ordinary refusal or negation is easily translated by 'No', 'Non', 'Nein', 'Nyet', and so on, according with the foreign language. But when the expanding phrases are employed so that they carry along with them a sub-surface connotation, then it is time for the interpreter to take over. So, when an American says '... not the chance of a snowball in hell', the vivid sense goes beyond negation. And, properly, it is the interpreter rather than the translator who should give it full scope, and thus supply both the context and character of the phrase.

Interpretation

Interpretation differs from translation because of its purpose. The function of interpretation is to explain what has been said; and the kind of explanation that will meet the situation depends on the depth of the interpreter's sense of vocabulary, grammar, syntax, and relevant usage. One man's interpretation can vary as widely as one man's ability to conduct a symphonic work. The comparison between linguistic and musical interpretation is just not only because so much rests on the conductor's skill in rendering the text of the musical work — but because the substance of the text makes reality as much from what he hears, what he chooses to emphasize, what he determines to understate.

In this regard, the conductor closely approaches the interpreter. For it is the duty of both to give body to the text of the communication, linguistic or musical, while portraying the sentiment of the composer.

Interpreters of language have the responsibility for communicating the spirit of the spoken or written word. They do more by way of addition of subtraction than do translators. In no way does their work disparage that of translators. Each has a separate task, even though the popular understanding assumes them to be one and the same in the way they act to render ideas intelligible interchangeably in two or more tongues.

Interpreters present the participants with more than mere linguistic equivalents. They can and do suggest the emotion of a text, and often accompany their interpretations with whatever gestures, grimaces and attitudes will impress the other side with their principal's character and feelings.

Within reasonable limitations, they can shade what is said, they can insert useful pauses, they can supplant periphrasis in one language with appropriate easy equivalents in another. They literally act as the ngeotiator's mouthpiece; and what they say must show him through their personalities. Thus it is important that interpreters, in place of being colourless as translators should be, ought to have an impressive manner of address, one that adds to the stature of their principal, or at the least, one that makes his presence compatible with the nature of the transaction. The constructions put forward by the ideal interpreter should convey perfectly the principal's concepts. The opposing side's concepts should be received by the interpreter and faithfully reduced to the cultural comprehension of the negotiator. Ideally, the interpreter at any international exchange stands almost on a par with his principal.

It is therefore extremely important for the negotiator to regard his choice of interpreter as critical to his foreign conversations. And, as a negotiator, he must be ready to have a 'strong' interpreter at his side. Merely taking the book-meaning of the foreign words does not suit the purpose; the interpreter, realistically, should be able to blend his principal's culture and character into the *verbatim* text, without altering the textual significance. And the interpreter's participation must be carefully controlled by the negotiator. Occasionally, the interpreters are literally carried away by their roles and often place themselves in amusing competition with their opposite numbers while the principals on both sides stand mute until the fury and fervour abate.

It is not amiss here to note the recognition given to interpreters of outstanding talent. One company's trebled export achievements were held to be consequent upon the successful interpretations provided by their director in charge of foreign trade. The company's receipt of a Queen's Award was said by the chief executive of Munton & Fison to be linked to the director's ability to speak a number of foreign languages, coupled with his knowledge of the culture and of the history of the various countries wherein the company was active. Interpreters hold the key to contract negotiations abroad; and their capacity for setting the climate for the negotiator and his foreign adversary should not be underrated, or deemed unworthy of careful attention. In fact, were interpreters chosen with full realization of their actual participating use, many foreign dealings would be commenced on a sounder and more satisfactory basis. The initial hostility between the negotiator and his foreign adversary would be buffered by the the intercession of the interpreter. In actual practice, many negotiators who have a high degree of fluency in a foreign language prefer to have an interpreter at the negotiation. The mechanical effect of the interpreter's function, screening, as it must, the negotiator from direct conversation, allows him to observe the adversary more carefully than he would had he to reply to questions immediately.

Needless to say, there are negotiators who neither know nor care about interpreter-functions. They feel confident of themselves at any negotiation, anywhere, anytime, in any language, irrespective of their total — or partial — ignorance of the foreign language, of the foreign culture, and of the foreign hostility to their presence and purpose. They believe it a show of bold courage to go it alone. Sometimes they reach contract abroad; more often they do not.

Semantics

Seen practically, semantics concern negotiators because they can be useful aids to communication in foreign transactions. When the negotiator has something to say, and that something may be too harsh in its impact, or too direct a personal comment, then he should be able to resort to circumlocution of a kind that will not disturb the negotiating atmosphere. But the semantic refuge should be left to the interpreter, for he — far better than the negotiator — will be in a position to work out an appropriate euphemism that can suit the necessity of the occasion.

Sometimes the semantic device is bi-planar; that is to say, the negotiator has to say something on one innocuous level, while implying some more dramatic theme on another. Obviously, one must be fairly cautious in finding a foreign semantic equivalent for 'I'll make you an offer you can't refuse'. When the English negotiator's 'I am so *very* sorry' requires a foreign equivalent, something more than literal accuracy should be discovered. For the English negotiator actually is saying (a) that he is not interested in the foreign terms of trade, and (b) that he will not modify his own offer.

The American 'I'll think it over' is neither a refusal nor a promise to consider a proposal. Somewhere between the two, it actually leaves the door open to an improved proposal. Here, too, the foreign phrase should be shaded accurately. The Spanish dilatory 'manana' can be taken any way — but almost never literally. It is a polite adjournment without a date pending the arrival of sufficient inducement to consummate the transaction. Everything semantic ties into the character of the foreigner. The Russian 'no' is never to be taken as a first and final refusal. It is a protective locution, emerging from traditional cultural negativism and political caution. It also is an invitation to sit down and pursue the particulars of the offer. Taking this kind of 'no' thus, the negotiator must be able to deal with the Russian response to his own 'no' issued when they offer him some terms, conditions or invitations to do business. The Slavic assumption is that the initial 'no' is in fact a negotiating overture, so the American — or English — early evidence of a disinclination to negotiate is rarely accepted literally, at least not by Russians or their Slavic brothers.

Hair splitting is a form of semantics that finds its way to the surface when the foreign side officially cannot accept a formal proposal as stated, but is willing to have it phrased while keeping the offer alive. Thus, in the case of an original proposal rejected by the foreign side because it imposed charges for interest and penalties for late payment, the negotiator was able to have his interpreter give the offer a new face by stating that the foreign company was being extended a 90-day credit, free of interest and penalty; but charges for interest and administration of the credit would attach on a per diem basis after the expiry of the 90-day credit period. Similarly, where the foreign company insisted on being able to designate the port of delivery for its goods, the negotiator was able to hold the bargain together by a judicious selection, through his interpreter, of words and phrases that did not negate the foreign company's right of designating the delivery port, but limited its choice of port to any of three on a short list prepared by the negotiator. The outcome was the same, but respect was given to the foreign adversary's 'face', to his company's official position, and to the spirit of negotiating compromise prevalent during the transaction.

Semantic selectiveness can not only minimize needless arguments and disputes, it can reduce their incidence. In essence semantic avoidance of abrasion is achieved by the 'half-full' or 'half-empty' option. The negotiator can usually choose the kind of positivism that will encourage the promotion of the foreign transaction; and he should instruct his interpreter to find the affirmative phrases in the foreign language that will execute the positive view, rather than those that may lead to a negative or inconclusive reception.

As an example, having due deference for the French hypersensitivity to their *amour propre*, the negotiator's proposal to invest money in a French venture was not made contingent upon proof of French 'good faith'. Rather it stated that the negotiator's company would make an initial advance of money to match the French contribution, and that each French contribution up to a sum certain would be met by the American equivalent in U.S. dollars.

International business does not find any constructive use for perjoratives during the negotiating phases; and the negotiator ought to be very careful about them. Too careless a resort to negative terminology can lead to litigation based on injuries to reputation; and a profitable business prospect ought to be kept free of extravagant language. The best rule for the negotiator to follow is that of constant caution, with a pretest of the language he wants transmitted by his interpreter.

One thing must be guarded against by the negotiator. While on foreign soil, there is an atrocious lack of restraint in using the loal language loosely. Somehow, we feel that we will be forgiven our singular sins of linguistics omission and commission. And, we are, often enough — especially when we venture to use the foreign language for social purposes.

But when it comes down to negotiating language, we fail to distinguish between our ineptitude and the requirements for doing business. Worse, having absorbed some local words and phrases, we assume they are about the same as our own locutions, and we inject them carelesly — and leave our foreign adversary annoyed, or amused, at our blunder. For example, we are keen on phrases like the American 'lock, stock and barrel' when we wish to speak of a buy-out, or some approximating totality. 'Whole bag of tricks', or the 'whole shooting match', can be used with like satisfaction as a graphic lively image. However, in picking up the odd bit of Chinese, of which we may be excessively proud, we learn that 'dung-shi', meaning 'east-west', is a word that means 'thing'; we take the east-west implication to mean 'everything'. This only partly so; for the word connotes that which is everything low, everything contemptible, everything worthless. We are brought up short, one way or another, when we refer to an object as an all-in-all, the last word, by fixing it with the Chinese 'dung-shi'. Our oriental counterpart's elevated eyebrows register amazement, not admiration, at our comment on the object that attracted our attention. It was one of his more elegant works of ceramic art.

The negotiator's willingness toward social congeniality does not necessarily require him to exhibit his bits and pieces of foreign words and phrases. The foreign courtesy may be mistakenly assumed to be approval, simply because he is neither reproved nor corrected for his linguistic impropriety. One exception might be noted. The French, whatever their gallantry elsewhere, are notoriously incapable of suffering an assault on the beauty of their spoken language. Their reverential pride for the spoken language is such that even amongst themselves they are constantly on the lookout for any threat to the purity of what, for them, is the loveliest, the most highly developed, the most perfect means of communication known to man — and they treasure the French language even more because it is spoken by the French alone as it should be. To impose upon their sensitivity a phrase like the dimly recollected school-boy translation of 'the pen of my aunt is on the table' can incur undying enmity and kill the deal.

Nuances

The negotiator's human *vade mecum* in charge of interpretation should be left free from interference. Having been selected for his competence, the negotiator should rarely quarrel with his work. Certainly in those instances where the negotiator has, rightly or not, the feeling that his aide is wrong, the best practice is to take up the matter at a convenient adjournment. If the word is referable to something of no consequence, it is wiser to overlook the matter — or await a coffee break. It is both bad practice and bad form to air the difference of opinion in the presence of the foreign side. For it serves only to give the adversary a later opportunity to say that he has been misunderstood, or that the interpreter is incompetent. Nuances are central to a shade of meaning; the shame can be carried by a phrase, or it can be expressed by tone or inflection of voice. On the assumption that the interpreter's understanding of his principal's purpose and personality is mature, it is usually advisable to leave it to his own judgment as to how a phase in the foreign language will reflect unconcern, or indifference, or confidence, or sincere intentions, or the negotiator's attractive idiosyncracies. It is almost impossible to make perfect interpretation from English into utterly different speech forms. The grammatical structures are barriers that can be reduced by approximations. And the extraordinary wealth of English simply is not found in other tongues. Some of them, like Chinese, have no articles. Some, like Russian, suffer from a short supply of synonyms. This field is fertile ground for etymologists. For our purposes it is enough to say that nuances in English may not exist in other languages, and the negotiator ought not to strain after gnats. If his interpreter conscientiously and capably sets out the communications clearly, that is a signal achievement. Nuances can be left to supplemental mechanics, physical for the most part, but nonetheless useful, (e.g. struggling, winkling, etc.).

In fact, it is common negotiating experience abroad that the nuances, if they play any major part in the transaction, make their appearance most often during the discussions of works of art, technicalities and legalisms; and since these most logically fall within the competence of specialists, it should be their particular responsibility and task to agree on what, if any, word or phrase is to be included — and what is to be left out of the preliminary memoranda reflecting the agreement.

Verbalization

Without doubt, placing our thoughts into words and sounding the words can be regarded as the most convenient of communication in conventional circumstances. Withal, most of us flesh out our verbalizations with something more, some physical act that provides a subsidiary significance to what we actually say. Even more, our verbalizations can be, and frequently are, contradicted by our physical acts, whether or not we intend them to be. On many occasions, we deliberately repudiate our words by gestures, grimaces, and physical movements. On other occasions, especially during foreign business, we do so involuntarily. Nevertheless, precise verbalization follows the main current of our thinking and feeling, and that of our foreign adversary. So it is only sensible that we examine our vocal instruments in order to check up on the extent that they aid or deter our communication. The hostility, xenophobic for the most part, that greets us also inspects us minutely. Part of the inspection deals with how we appear when we are saying something in what—to the other side—is a foreign language. We may be unaware of our verbalizing patterns. Our stutterings, our vocal backings and fillings, our mumblings, our head-held asides to the interpreter give off an aura of furtiveness that runs against our own sight of ourselves. We, for instance, see ourselves as modest, deferential, polite, and painfully ready to catch the every word of our foreign adversary. He observes us as wrapped in secrecy, occupied with some purpose contrary to his company's interests. We smile ingratiatingly; he takes it as a small gloating in anticipation of our later victory. We sit hunched forward; he sees us as tense, poised, ready to pounce upon him. Verbalization states the major theme of our business abroad. It should be unimpeded by physical contradictions — save where we mean to show our feelings at odds with our words. Thus, in speaking of a competitor, when we say we are sorry for his misfortune but simultanesouly roll our eyes heavenward in cynical amusement, we will be safely discreet while unmistakeably delighted at whatever disastrous destiny awaits him.

The French shoulder-shrug is universally understood, but it is understood differently by those who see it. For instance, does it mean lack of information on a point in question? Or is it to be taken as lack of interest in a settled matter? Or does our French adversary decline to respond to our query? Or does he attempt a silent denigration?

Assuming for the moment that the French uses of various kinds of shoulder-shrugging are, at least to them, fairly explicit, they most certainly are not to us. But we agreed to leave nuances to our interpreters, and that must suffice.

What is of cardinal interest in verbalization lies in two concepts. The first is that verbalization abroad is only part of the context of communication running between us and our foreign adversary. The other part is physical. Both parts comprise the foreign message-sending apparatus. Both parts are to be read together, so to speak, in order for us to draw and understand the picture in its entirety, stating what the mental and emotional makeup of our foreign adversary is.

The next point is that verbalization is the prime means for stimulating ideas. Forgetting for the moment what effect is produced by supplemental physical phenomena, it is verbalization, the use of words and phrases to stir our foreign adversary, that must be effectually employed by us through our interpreter. And correspondingly, we should be able to hear, diagnose and respond — or restrain our responses — to the words and phrases sent us by the foreign adversary.

The focus of our attention on verbalization is critical to any successful approach to persuasion. In order for us to convince our foreign adversary of the merits of our offer, we must verbalize a good portion of our position when we confer with him. It may well be true that our presence will be itself impressive, or that our papers will lay out our proposals adequately, or that his necessity will compel his accession to our terms. But, as a general rule, it is what we say that will impinge on his conscious will, drawing him to us — or, if we mistake what is to be done, repelling him from us.

If our foreign adversary cannot be stirred to agreement by what we say, by our logical — if he is the sort to whom logic is important — approach, or by the rationality of our argumentation, if, as often is the case rationality is acceptable, then we ought to hold no false hope of bringing our business to a happy conclusion. Verbalization by us as well as verbalization toward us, issuing from the other side, must be prepared and engaged as the operative means of bringing into play our repertoire of psychological techniques meant to persuade the other side of our proposal's merits. Whatever is necessary should be done to polish up our verbalizations. Whatever we have to say, directly or through our interpreters, should be said well — and often enough, during the foreign negotiation so that our position is established.

Pauses

Rolling rhetoric is part and parcel of familiar after-dinner orations, fraternal eulogies, and purple sales pitches. American and English business men, allowing for national variations, know the patterns of commemorative address, political campaign perorations, and pushcart persuasions. Who has not heard and seen the trade association member 'point with pride', the trade union rouser 'view with alarm', the public officials 'agonizing soul-searching', and the thousand and one sound-and-sight cliches that have fed the hopes and fears of the American and English Community for years. We know the outstretched arm, the upraised hand, the profiled head, the glassy smile, and the full scale of practised charm. We have become accustomed to the gamut of grimace. What we have not noticed with equal keenness is the interspersed pause. The deliberate moment of silence plays upon us imperceptibly quickening our pulse while paralyzing our analytical processes, so that we wait for the dramatic arrival of the moment of truth. The wellspring of rebellious thought is dry. We stand on our emotional tip-toes, enthralled, raptured, and intellectually stranded. We have been hooked. That our expectations are disappointed matters little. The pause prepared us for something else, some revelation.

In foreign negotiation, the event to watch out for is the foreign pause. Sometimes it is accompanied by a steady gaze, sometimes by a covert, sidelong glance to see how far gone we are. Sometimes, indeed, we are ignored as if absent, while the foreign adversary looks into the distance beyond the walls of the office where we are conferring. We found ourselves waiting again; we have been taken in by the portentous pause, and its effect is more powerful because it was preceded by the unceasing foreign voice incanting something that we have only partly understood through our interpreter. Like the hypnotic trance that transfixes the chicken before the snake, we come to a halt. The foreign cadence, the foreign voice, the foreign illogic and contrariness are rendered powerful through the foreign pause. Stale, banal, all too familiar to us, in our own stamping grounds, when we are abroad we are ensnared by the pause again, not by reason of our ready susceptibility but because of the alien skill in whetting our curiosity with a torrent of words that, however strange and meaningless to our untutored ears, resemble the auctioneer's drum-beat patter. The sudden cessation holds us fascinated in the spell of sudden silence while the speaker surveys us, and waits assured of his eventual success.

Pauses in foreign speech are unlike our own. We halt when we are at a temporary loss for words. Foreigners pause for dramatic effect; they have built up the scene toward a moment of emotional tension. Their control of pause is deliberate and not to be taken as a flight from vocalization because of lack of self-assurance. Rather, it is a species of oratorical probe, not too different in purpose from the housewife's insertion of a fork into the flesh of a turkey, testing whether it has been cooked enough. The foreign speech pattern reaches into our credulousness. And we ought to appreciate its purpose clearly.

One way to turn the foreign pause to our own advantage is to make an early assessment of the foreigner's rhythm. No matter what language he uses, an intelligent listener can discern the regularity, note the irregularity caused by the interruptions, and assign to them some logical function. Whether the pause is plainly intended to see how far we will be prepared to swallow a statement, or to vote our immediate reactions, every pause abroad is part of a speech pattern. Having an interpreter near us is of immense value; in addition to telling us what has been said and how it ought to be understood, he allows us to do what the Chinese refer to as 'look-look'. This is a more penetrating observation than 'look-see'. We can observe more critically. If we are alert, we can relate the pause to a succeeding exaggeration, and thus establish a kind of oratorial periodicity that should be treated with care.

In speaking to the point of foreign speech patterns, we are stressing the importance of conscious observation devoted to a psychological tell-tale. Later on in our discussion we shall deal with psychological techniques. But such techniques to which we have been enured at home, both as practitioners and subjects, succeed in direct relationship to the negotiator's awareness of behavioural characteristics in communication; and a pause is an important characteristic, not only with respect to the general style of presentation used by the foreign adversary but for the reason that we can seize it as an opportunity to break into his presentation. This breaking is a means for disorganizing both his presentation and his preconceived plan of persuasion, while, simultaneously, it lays him open to what we have constructed as a method of convincing him toward agreement. To paraphrase a theatrical axiom, every little foreign pause has a meaning of its own; and it is our job to know what that meaning is in terms of psychologically sound persuasion.

Non-verbalization

The absolute and comparative importance of verbalized communication has been mentioned, and together with it a sufficient hint of the relevance of gestures and associated physical movements has been supplied. But, taking a further look at non-verbalization, we shall appreciate its function in foreign business negotiations more clearly. The pause, of which something was said in the preceding paragraphs, is, so to speak, the tip of the non-verbalizing iceberg. Going beyond it, anyone who has witnessed a miming performance cannot fail to be favourably impressed by the actor's skill in attracting the audience's attention, inducing its cooperation, and illuminating by physical movement a story, or an incident that evokes an emotional response in all who are present.

When, as often we do, stand near a cluster of foreigners animatedly talking to each other, our amusement at the arm-waving, the finger-pointing, the head-turning, the body-swaying and the walking to and fro is tinged with a slightly disparaging superciliousness. We believe it a sign of social inferiority when people resort to broad movements rather than to speech that can be heard. We forget that we are as much drawn by the visible as much, and likely more, as by the audible proofs of communication. We go abroad and discover that the non-verbal demonstrations are, after all, very useful. We, after a short stay, find ourselves using them enthusiastically because our command of the foreign language is limited. At the same time, we are educating ourselves in the art of understanding body language, snorts, scissor-like hand-cuttings of the air, grunts and groans come, sooner than we think, to signify, and in doing so wear a different dignity—one we have learned to share.

This is a step in the right direction. We have graduated from a somewhat perplexed condescension toward a new evaluation of the emotional evidences of what the foreigner is thinking or feeling deep within himself; and these emotional signs are precisely what the negotiator must perceive and read while he is abroad. Not only are they vital to his sense of how his foreign adversary responds, but they are clues as to how to bring out his responses, how to stimulate his cultural reactions, how to reach him across the conceptual distances. Some ideas are merely universal and go together with purely physical movements. Others are particularly local and require explication that is verbal. For such as can be communicated readily, foreigners are just as apt to use the physical movement exclusively.

American and English negotiators are aware that political as well as social distinctions exist in non-Western countries; that the expression of divergent, not to mention dissident views, can be dangerous; and that the consequences of such expressions can be damaging in many ways. Granted this, non-verbalization takes on functions that must be understood as required by the time, place and circumstance found abroad. Not least of the functions is political and personal security. Thus, shoulder-shrugging, up-turned palms, mouth-pursing and the thousand and one other signals that are unvoiced abroad have become part of the social necessity for self-preservation. Non-verbalization is not to be criticised as a crude form of communication inherent in foreigners and attributable to their lack of social grace.

Non-verbalized communication varies with the ethnic community, and, within it, with the several kinds of social organization that comprise the regulators of community life. On foreign soil, the negotiator must find out the distinctions of non-verbalization as they apply to himself and to his foreign adversary. It may be correct for his opposite number to grimace, gesticulate and shout; while, at the same time it is not in order for the negotiator to do so. The Armenian may say 'yes' by nodding his head without voicing a syllable. The Arabian may indicate assent by looking straight at the negotiator, while stroking his own face in search for blemishes later to be dealt with. In Austria we may be misled by a variety of perpetual motion that seems to spell agreement; this is accomplished by a series of rapid head-noddings, joined to an ineradicable smile that encourages our remarks however made in stumbling German. The open-eyed silent acquiesence in what we are saying is irresistable. In fact, many foreigners know how to flatter our egos by adopting the most deferential physical attitudes that spell 'yes'. Only later to we learn that our massaged vanity misinterpreted the non-verbalization for what we wished it to be. On our parts, we must accept non-verbalization, whatever form it takes, as indigenous and untransportable. The grin in Dublin is not the same as that in Belfast. The smile in Spain is quite different from that in Santo Domingo. And if we feel the need for becoming non-verbalizing communicators, then we must suit our grimace to the place. Our physiognomic correspondence to our foreign adversary in Lisbon must not be extended to Bonn. And this limitation applies with equal force to other physical forms of communication.

Physical signs and symbols

If only because he must adapt himself to a totally new cultural environment, the negotiator of international business has a harder task than his domestic market counterpart. From our earlier years we have acquired a facility in inducing others to do what we wish them to do. This ease of persuasion relates partly to our personal talents, and partly to the social position we hold. Enforced by some special authority issuing from our official rank, civil or military, we move others from indifference toward or away from some act. The effort entailed in the performance of an act, or in restraining oneself from doing it, is recognized as a physical exertion that must be measured in terms of expended energy. The proof of such a physical conception is supplied by our language. We apply 'muscle'; or, alternatively, we 'sweat out' amiably or impatiently a change of circumstance. We regard perspiration as an evidence of human response. Physiologically, we believe, the effort-factor may be equated by the perspiration-product. So, when our foreign adversary tells us something false, we look for signs of his physical discomfort. A witness under cross-examination by counsel is expected to 'pale', to 'redden', to 'turn ashen', to 'blush', to 'flush', to 'purple', to squirm, wring his hands, stir uneasily, hunch his shoulders, shift his position, drum his fingers, twist his ankles, fumble with his jacket, and, of course, to sweat buckets of guilt-symbolizing fluid. The fact of the matter is that the classic witness reaction of wrongdoing. And the culpable criminal sits calm, composed, cool and immobile, fending off queries with all of the exterior signs of self-confidence. This leaves us at a loss at home when we are dealing with a domestic adversary whose skulking manner excites our suspicions and destroys our analytical prowess when we find out, too late, that he is a paragon of private virtues and the repository for all public esteem.

How much more involved is our work abroad when, so far as we know (despite our liberal educations) one foreigner is like another? How can we learn the differences between those who are trustworthy and those who are not; or between those who are dependable and those who are not; or between those who mean to do business and those who do not; and, most importantly, between those who will succumb to us and those who will not? If we undertake to 'play it by ear', we may find the tune jarring. In other words, body movements must be understood with respect to the negotiating climate. If in the United States hand-shaking markes the candid, courageous virile male, in France it is an insufferable invasion of social privacy unless exchanged between equals or near-equals. England regards hand-clasps as a variety of initial recognition; once is enough. The Germans go in for a vigorous arm pumping. The Russians do too, but they keep their arms stiff — and preserve all of the physical implications of 'arms-length dealings'. The Scandinavians, allowing for fine distinctions amongst Swedes, Danes and Norwegians, use the hand-shaking as a test of physical strength; they still hold a primitive veneration for raw power. Italy enjoys body-touching, hand-on-thigh contacts, shoulder-rubbing, arm-linking fraternal saunterings and, appropriate to the occasion, kissing. But this latter non-verbalization must be carefully distinguished; the Sicilian kiss differs in purpose and consequence from the one in Milan. In France, body-language is egocentrically consecrated to expressing the personality. Fingers are waved or raised in paired signs of warning. Eyes roll up, veer to the side, and mate with poutings, chin-pointings and cheek-puffing in order to speak or outrage, conditions impossible to meet, and cynicism too impolite to be set into words.

Non-verbalization is suggestive. Whether or not it is declaratory of the foreign adversary's intention is beside the mark. What is important is that his movements be followed, and then classified usefully for their psychological meaning. Of course, body movements, or any other form of communication, can be simulated in order to falsely portray the mood and motives of the opposite side. And too often this is done so expertly, so successfully that we have to force ourselves to disregard what we see and hear in favour of what we think we see and hear. More than this, we have to discard our classic notions of what an open countenance is, what a steady stare conveys, what a shifty-eyed person's character truly is, and what foreigners are like.

By analogy, and based on the basic assumption that human nature is fundamentally moved by circumstances, and that human communications reflect circumstances, mood and meaning, we resort to a sometimes mystic construction placed on non-verbal communications. Often enough we are mistaken. But we have no option; we cannot ignore what we see any more than we can what we hear. Both verbalization and non-verbalized communication must be analyzed as quickly and as accurately as possible, and then reduced to their useful functions in foreign business.

Physical signs seen from their positive side aid the expression of communicating language. Taken together with verbal forms, or independently, they can be used to transmit ideas and, as well, to receive them. As an example, at auctions held abroad there are many conventional signs, suited to the items made the subject of the sale, that without a word show the bidder's willingness to buy and the price he is prepared to pay. Distaste can be expressed by nose-wrinkling. Head-nodding during a negotiation abroad is familiar means for continuing the conversation while, in the absence of verbal confirmation, omitting particular proof of consent. The American 'I yessed him to death' head-nodding is well known; and so are the Continental forms. Down-turned mouth corners are physical evidence of negation, or disapproval. So-called sparkling eyes are signs of elation, joy, approval or interest; they also communicate eagerness, avidness, and affectionate regard. Actually, during any negotiation, it is possible to make a quick study of the opposite side and find out what the 'sending' code of physical signs consists of. And in international business, the negotiator soon acquaints himself with the particular code-identification of his foreign adversary. What is difficult for him is to find a 'sending' code that will assist him in transmitting what he wishes to communicate while not revealing what he wishes to hold secret.

To treat all the physical signs within the human range of expression lies beyond this discussion. What might be stated is that whether it is opened through a form of doodling, or by excessive perspiration, or by tossing a coin, or toying with a watch chain, communication of a sort — even contrary to what is made apparent by means of verbalization — the interior stew of emotional and intellectual action and reaction tends to show itself through physical signs; and when they are read correctly, it is possible for the negotiator to use them profitably.

From what was earlier said, it must be apparent that the negotiator who seeks an insight into the operations of his foreign adversary's mind should remember that those operations are largely, if not entirely, responses to the adversary's cultural background and influences. And insofar as they have a direct or indirect bearing on what the adversary reveals and the manner in which it is revealed, the negotiator must possess a fairly correct appraisal of the foreign cultural factors. Some of them can be deduced easily by observing casually what the proverbial man-in-the-street is like. Others are found in the cinema, the theatre, the television and stage productions. The local literature, especially detective stories, can be useful.

Symbolism holds much of value for the international negotiator because it affords him a sight of how his foreign adversary thinks of himself. The adversary usually knows the effect of his symbol and means to use the symbol as a badge of social status, professional qualification, official authority, academic attainment, or even seniority, or commonly as a mark of affluence. Thus, sapphire cuff-links, gold tie-pins, an elaborately worked watch-chain, or a costly cigar-case, can bespeak the owner's taste, good or bad (usually he sees himself as having good taste; if there is any doubt, he passes off the article as a gift he is bound to display, however reluctantly). Again, button-hole decorations, such as flowers, are certainly intended to show a sense of the exquisite. While those that are enamelled with a club shield are meant to speak of the wearer's affiliations with a power-group of one kind or another. Medals need no explanation as such; in fact, whenever they are worn, one may tae it as a measure of the wearer's lack of self-assurance that he must put forward his credentials; this kind of wearing of status on the sleeve should be understood as calling for finesse. For the negotiator may justifiably assume that his foreign adversary's self-esteem will be brought to the fore whenever a difference of opinion rises or a fact is challenged. The medal-wearer is amongst the foremost exponent of the ruffled 'Are you questioning *my* good faith'? expostulation.

Whatever open symbol is shown, it has a meaning. And the negotiator ought to take note of it as early as possible. It is meant to be seen; it is meant to be mentioned; and it is meant to be the source of question/answer colloquy. If the negotiator appreciates this to be so, he can win his way to his adversary's heart by admiring the badge, listening to the explanation, and complimenting the wearer. Flattery, subtly laid on, goes farther than factual exposition in winning a sympathetic ear.

Symbols known within a social enclave need no explanation. All who see them know their message. But the negotiator need not hesitate; after all he is an outsider, and if he wishes to be seen as impressionable he can do better than appear naively impressed. At once he himself will be seen as a person of taste, intelligence, and discretion. His query will be respected as one prompted by courteous curiosity; and the door to contract-formation will open wider than it would had he overlooked what he had been intended to see and speak of. Signals must be understood as somewhat different from symbols and signs. By way of an example, when we play tennis we watch our opponent's position at the base line in order to see what his probable serving strategy will be. We look at his feet, at his body's inclination toward the box — or away from it — to which he must serve. We notice the circling of his racket over his head in order to discover whether he will slice his serve. If our eyes are keen enough, we look at his grip on the handle of the racket, and deduce from its being Western or Eastern just what we may expect by way of a forehand drive or an overhand smash. So it is in our foreign negotiation. Our adversary's constant reference to statistical reports may be a signal of his lack of generalized information, or of a poor briefing, or of an unfamiliarity with the actual operative features of the transaction. On the other hand, it may be his way of trying to steam-roller us with citations of authoritative material.

In some cases, the massing of impressive material is self-defeating. If, for example, our Domestic Company is ready to appoint Foreign Company as local agent in Ruritania, we do not require certifications of Foreign Company's track record on behalf of other companies. They add nothing to our knowledge, and only make us inquisitive as to what Foreign company may be withholding from view.

Signals in foreign business should be understood as flags waving on the road to our foreign adversary's character. Whatever he does will be consistent with the signals we have read, and with his own predisposition. If the signals are inconsistent with our readings of his character, then we must take them for feints and false leads and guide ourselves accordingly. The way to get a good working impression of our foreign adversary is to see him first as an individual — and then as a social unit. In either role his 'signals' must be in line with who he is and what his character is; and, additionally, as a social unit, he must conform his conduct to his official function. In this light, assuming we are oriented to his cultural background, all we need do is balance his consistent conduct against such signals as may be out of character. They are the ones that can lead to mistake, errors of judgment, or deception; and when they show themselves we must be prudent enough to halt long enough to reorganize our estimate of our foreign adversary, and also to reform our negotiating tactics.

Although it is easy to tell the reader to watch out for, observe, and then act on foreign signals, it is impossible to tell him the nature of any given set of foreign signals without correlating the signals to the cultural features of the country within which he will be doing his foreign business. What the negotiator can do abroad, apart from consulting with a local psychologist with respect to local motivations, signals and conduct, is to return fundamental incentives and impulses. People tend to act in answer to emotional stimuli. True the form of their responses may be intellectualized, but at the bottom what they do is set in motion by how they feel. And for our purposes we may be safe in taking it as a fact that love, hate, hunger and fear are the great categories for human feeling; that these categories are known stimuli wherever man exists; and that his reactive movements to these stimuli may be expressed within his cultural framework. Where the framework takes precedence over his individual initiative, as within the Eastern Bloc countries, we ought to expect to find that his signs, symbols and signals are restrained; and, as a matter of fact they are. The Slavic philosophy of individual suppression in favour of the needs of the State ensures that little if any opportunity for personal expression exists. All that the Slavic negotiator is capable of within his philosophical existence is the expression of those communicating forms that manifest a desire to supply the needs of the State.

This means that the negotiator ought to limit his approach to the Slavic adversary within the bounds of possibility. Additionally, he should not mistake the signs, symbols and signals as overtures to personal contacts, or as evidence of personal incentives. The Slavic negotiator exists only to execute the State plan so far as it falls within the periphery of his official function. On the other hand, where the negotiator is free to deal with foreign negotiators on the basis of their personal ambitions, expectations, drives and incentives, he must look out for the signs, symbols and signals that indicate the pulse of the adversary, and the centres of his susceptibility; read accurately, the negotiator can make a fairly educated guess as to what will be personally attractive to his foreign adversary. This is subject only to the logical rule that the foreign adversary's personal views must broadly correspond with his cultural ones. Experienced negotiators know this well enough, and aim their appeals toward a coincidence of cultural and personal purpose.

Signals are not abstractions. They radiate an identification of the foreign adversary that can be used to good advantage. According to his nature, he can be dealt with by convincing him that the proposed transaction will (a) benefit his company, and (b) advance his position within the company. In this context, (b) constitutes a reward or prize. Stated in other terms, the benefits to the foreign negotiator and to his company tends to satisfy company requirements and personal ones. Thus the foreign adversary's position is safeguarded by the coincident benefits. The statement that 'What is good for General Motors is good for the country', becomes agreeably particularized insofar as the transaction's benefits proportionately accrue to the foreign negotiator.

While we have mentioned the signals received from the foreign adversary, it is essential to make the point that the negotiator must see to it that signals run from him to the other side. However the signals are made to appear, they must evidence (a) his power to act affirmatively, (b) his willingness to do so. He must especially signal his understanding of the foreign company's requirements, and, in conjunction with them, his understanding of the foreign adversary's need to bring off some coup, some proof of success that will enhance his prestige within the foreign company.

Since the affirmative signals should be clear and unmistakable, the negotiator can point out the specific advantages to be gained by the foreign company, and, simultaneously, he can motivate his foreign adversary by looking at the likelihood of promotion, pecuniary profit, and personal preferment. This comes down to an adaptation of the General Motors concept for the purpose of the transaction. For, by opening up the foreign adversary's eyes to the coincidence of his interest with that of his company as respects the business in hand, he heightens the motivation for positive action on the part of the foreign adversary. In order words, the negotiator's signal apparatus must receive from the foreign adversary some message showing the latter's motivation; and, in return, the negotiator should signal his power and purpose to satisfy it.

The negotiator's outgoing signals are in effect a promise that will be contingent on the cultural background of the foreign adversary, the official role he plays, the individual authority he has, and the consideration required to convert his hostility to amicability. The negotiator must also protect the foreign adversary from embarrassment in the event of premature investigation and disclosure; and he must signal his ability to do this.

Attitudes and immobility

If we understand attitude to be the reaction to a situation, then it is clear that all of the communicating instruments of the negotiator are brought forward in order to create an attitude, that of his foreign adversary, to the transactional situation. The negotiator's deployment of verbalization, non-verbalization, body communicators, signs, symbols and signals is meant solely and wholly to induce his adversary to adopt an attitude that will accept the terms and conditions required to promote the purpose of the foreign business.

Attitudes toward business, like those toward other conventional social relationships, are rooted in what the community structure regards as critical for its survival. This is another way of saying that cultural necessity is responsible for the kind of attitude that emerges from social interaction; whether that interaction be friendly or hostile, there is a vocabulary of attitude so to speak, that is generally adequate for the situation. Enlisted men salute officers as a conditioned attitude within a military situation. Yet, within the same situation, experienced veterans can impart to their salute, a disdain that makes second lieutenants shiver. Churchill's 'V' expressed a social attitude of defiance. De Gaulle's *hauteur* was the epitome of national pride. Hitler's harangues bespoke another national attitude; and Roosevelt's fireside chats still another. Market vendors have cozening attitudes that attract and detain their customers. Attitudes enfold all of the paraphernalia of communication, including pause and silence. The postures depicted by Daumier immortalized the attitudes taken by French tribunals, and French lawyers, to French litigants.

How we stand, sit, walk, talk, murmur, whisper can express our reactions, our attitudes, to the situations within which we must act. Every part of us is involved in expressing our attitude. And it understates the case to assume that oral communications alone suffice to present our feelings and thoughts. Something more is needed to round out the picture of who we are, from where we come and what we represent. We ourselves manufacture our personalities by how we act and react, physically, to other persons. Knowing this, at home we customarily present ourselves through attitudes. But when we are abroad we fail to appreciate the need to give our attitudes expressive forms suited to the foreign situation. So far as we are equipped to do so, we should see the point of presenting our attitudes in terms of the foreign culture. If we fail this, then we risk being misunderstood in our purpose.

And if we fail to see the foreign adversary's attitude as the product of his individual responses to his environment, to his experience within it, and to the range of cultural influence to which he has been subjected during his life, we risk misunderstanding him. Since it is we who journey abroad to do business, the duty of showing ourselves through attitudes appropriate to the foreign scene cannot be debated. Nor can our need to accept the foreign adversary's attitude as natural to him.

Furthermore, our ability to take in stride a Swedish negotiating attitude may help but does not ensure a like ability to deal with a business man from Belize. It would be plain error to do so, that is to assume that one foreigner resembles another hailing from a different country. We are often exasperated because of superficial resemblances in attitudes. The American smiling soft-sell approach ought not to be confused with the Japanese deferential smiling response. The Oriental apparent attitude of assent does not by any means signify that he (a) agrees, (b) that he understands, (c) that he is ready to trade. What it does mean within his own cultural mould is that he respects the persons (in this case ourselves) who address him; that he is habitually trained against giving open offense; that he reserves his decision for consultation with his superiors.

English social attitudes are carried over into business negotiations. It is good form to nod, to smile, to continue conversations and to encourage the social amenities. The attitude does not imply total, or even partial, acceptance of what is said. Russians nod vigorously, interrupt frequently, bide their moments for heated disputation, which they then interlard with anecdotes heir conversational attitude at formal negotiations is reserved, especially when they are negotiating as a team. Each nation has its negotiating attitude; and within the national pattern each foreign adversary adds his own personal touch.

What should the negotiator's attitude be, in the face of foreign negotiating attitudes? How should he let himself be seen. The simplest attitude, and the one that will be best received, is taken by showing himself as he genuinely is. If he is experienced in international business, he will know very quickly how to cultivate and promote an affiliative response from his foreign adversary. And he will be very careful to avoid transparent modifications that may give offense.

It is hopelessly difficult to attempt to state what the negotiator ought to do and how he should respond to every kind of foreign attitude. But it can only be helpful for him to learn something of the trends, tendencies and types of culture he will face within a specific foreign market. While it is unlikely that at first meeting he will bare his hopes, fears, dreams and illnesses to his foreign adversary, he nevertheless must accept as nonchalantly as he can the Mid-Easterner's readiness to discuss his latest medical reports, his earliest recollections of life at school, his unsuccessful efforts to unload a commodity surplus. The negotiator ought to see the confidence-exchange as habitual to the Mid-Easterner; and he should respond to it as gracefully as he can. Out West, in America, where the tradition holds that men are silent, strong, daring, bold, crafty, open-handedly generous, the attitude for a negotiation would be to strive for an instinctive accord from the first 'Yup'. In the Eastern Coastal States, a coming-on-strong negotiating attitude is standard. If we can think of foreign territories as regions that must be catered to because of cultural differences within our own national borders, then it should be simple enough to understand that once we leave the United States, or the United Kingdom, we must bow to the local negotiating attitude.

The immutable negotiating principle for international transactions is this: never, never, never open trading proposals until a personal bond is fixed between the negotiator and his foreign adversary. Collaterally, the negotiator should see to it from his first moment on foreign soil that his whole attitude is tuned to whatever the local sitution requires, expects and will accept. This does not necessitate obsequiousness. And as was earlier noted, it does not make the negotiator a party to local shenanigans. At the same time he is not to see himself as a self-appointed, self-anointed moralist sitting in judgment on the manners, customs and practices current at the foreign site. He may nod, sit wide-eyed, frown, utter timely 'Right's', and do anything that will connect him to his foreign adversary, excepting of course those things that he would find offensive to his own code of personal conduct. The main thing to be borne in mind is that the negotiator's attitude must be harmonious, must fit in with that of his foreign adversary, and must multiply the occasions for 'connections' that will culminate in contract.

Immobility

During most international business negotiations a time will come when the negotiator's urge to get the contract and go to the airport will rise to his head like an attack of swamp-fever. That is a dangerous moment. That is when he ought to sit still and let the urge pass. That is precisely when his 'take-charge' impulses must be stifled. That is when he should calmly assess his position, counting the plus and minus elements of the negotiation. And if the favourable points preponderate, he can push forward to contract. If not, then he ought to say nothing, remembering the Italian saying 'A closed mouth catches no flies'. The wrong word at the right time can be fatal. If the cards fall right, he has nothing to lose by immobility. If something goes amiss, his steadiness, his attitude of negotiating savoir faire, will see him over the lull, or impase, or whatever it is that ties up the forward movement or the deal. It is here that the German *sitzfleisch,* the capacity of sitting tight, proves an asset. On the other hand if he shows annoyance, he loses an inestimably important negotiating edge: mystery. So long as he resists impetuousness, he can seize the helm. These dismaying negotiating doldrums should not be allowed to show the negotiator as hypersensitive to inertia. Physical immobility costs nothing. As a matter of fact, Chinese and Japanese negotiators know how to capitalize on the atmosphere of suspense and agitation; indeed they are masters at taking the negotiation down to the wire and then halting the conversations, hoping to press the negotiator to a modification of the terms earlier agreed.

Greek, Italian, Spanish and French negotiators resemble the American breed in their impatience during the final stages. Sometimes they walk out dramatically, returning with new demands. In the end, the parties resume their course, the negotiation picks up steam and the negotiator's unruffled persistence pays dividends. He has preserved face; he has shown common sense; he has outlasted the needling harassment of foreign inaction; and, of course, he has not prejudiced his mission. His immobility under pressure has made it possible for him to take back a contract that will return a profit for his company's investment in the foreign transaction. For himself, he has avoided surrender to pique, while consolidating his successful negotiating experience. His success as an internationalist can only lead to further opportunity abroad, either within his company, or as an independent.

Chapter 7

Hints on international negotiation

Materials; presentations; time, place and circumstance; tempo, reorganization; personality problems; reality and fiction of hostility; community of interest; working with possibilities; rites, ceremonies and mutual respect

Foreign negotiations look to foreign sites. The negotiator should equip himself so that he can exert his psychological controls during the bargaining abroad. Wherever he goes, he should organize his expedition so that he has safe access and free agress; lodging, meals, local services, local transportation, communication with his company, secretarial assistance, taping and typing machines, contacts with consular, legal, banking, medical and dental offices, and necessary accreditation should be provided as a routine caution against misadventure. So far as possible, he ought to be self sufficient during his foreign mission; and, ideally, he should not permit himself to become obligated to his foreign adversary for favours that will limit his own freedom of movement and decision. He ought to anticipate the probabilities of surveillance, espionage and agressive acts intended to sabotage his efforts and thwart his company's purpose in the foreign market.

Materials

The negotiator should see himself as a theatrical director and undertake to furnish himself with whatever will implement the conduct of his transaction. Records, references, commercial forms, audio-visual devices, negotiating instructions, background documentation, statistical reports, even coloured tab-indexed notebooks might be thought of. If he will be host to the negotiating conference abroad, then he must be able to set up the essential catering, food, drink and tobacco amenities for the conferees. Moreover, power-supply for electronic instruments, Polaroid cameras, brochures, goodwill company gifts of pencils or similar items can form part of his negotiating tools. So far as they may affect or pertain to his business, he can look to provisions for press releases, newspaper coverage, market returns. For his purposes, he should see himself as a quarter-master in charge of all of the materials useful to his strategy and sufficient to prevent embarrassing failures of material or services. Above all, while on 'enemy' territory, he must be capable of offsetting the adversary's physical advantages of supply.

Negotiations abroad vary from each other. No foreign transaction is like another; there are too many factors that work their effects upon the business to be done at one place to permit it to follow the same path it would take at another. The negotiator's purpose is to 'capture' the site, to settle himself within it for however long he must be there. He should be ready to deal with the rival negotiators seeking entry in the same market. He should do everything to magnify his effort; and in this sense whatever will lend him an imposing presence should be considered when he prepares his materials. This is not a matter of egotism; he carries the flag, so to say, and the flag of his company must be equated with power. While he might do his negotiating under a naked light bulb in a railway station, or at an impromptu roadside cafe, he should work toward creating a strong first impression. The desiderata are (1) containing controversy, (2) establishing good personal 'connections' with his adversary, and (3) reaching contract. Whether he is en route from the airport, or on a factory floor, or beside an oilfield derrick, he must have whatever the circumstances suggest as essential for his stated objectives. He can profitably remember that 'packaging' his presentation adds to the attractiveness of his proposals and makes them more acceptable. How he 'packages' them is a matter of taste and intelligent adaptation to the foreign scene.

Presentation

The negotiator should treat his initial meeting with the foreign adversary as a kind of reconnaissance supported by a prefigured order of battle. He should estimate the character of the opposition, its strength, and the bargaining ploys available to it. Certainly the negotiator must look out for every early opportunity to dominate the conference. he entrance he makes should be planned for this end. Once within the office or conference room, he ought to measure his opposite number and make a swift judgment as to what kind of negotiating stance will be most effective.

Eye-movement patterns of the adversary should be noted, analyzed and converted into dominance-indicators. The negotiator can learn much from closely observing the eye-movements, the eyelid narrowings and widenings, the avoidance of eyeball to eyeball fastenings. Whatever he learns will stand him in good stead during the opening negotiating phase when he must overcome his adversary's hostility.

Presenting himself to best advantage, gaining dominance by eye-control, taking a strategic seat at the conference table are part of the ABC of negotiating tactics abroad as at home. After this exploratory control seems set, and the negotiator selects his line of approach, he can improve his 'friendly' attitude by unobtrusively leaving his head-of-the table chair in favour of one closer to his adversary. The gesture will not be lost, and the overture will be taken as intended — as a signal of 'equality'. This touch is most important in countries where national sensitivity is joined to personal apprehensions caused by differences in social rank and official position. The negotiator can go a step farther. He can leave the side of his adversary, sit on the table, dangling his leg casually, and then remove his jacket. American shirt-sleeve round-table democracy is much in vogue abroad. The 'let it all hang out' informality is greatly appreciated, especially in those new nations where striving for democracy begins with emulating the Americans as they are represented in the cinema. But the presentation of the 'American-in-Paris' can reverse the field by outdoing local pomp-and-circumstance displays. Naturally sometimes it is extremely useful to lay on the luxurious VIP treatment for the benefit of the adversary. Whichever approach to 'dominance' is followed, the progress toward a solid proof of 'community of interest', or 'connections', between himself and his adversary should be steady, unremitting and supported throughout the period of 'presentation'.

Depending on the early appraisal of the adversary, it lies

within the negotiator's discretion to present his business via a fast-paced audio-visual delivery, or its opposite — a soft, leisured, somewhat hesitant — even bumbling, demonstration. Allowing a sort of question period to be included can be helpful, particularly in countries where the foreign adversary's egotism might be quick to take offense if he is deprived of the occasion to question. Social standing counts for a great deal; and the negotiator must distinguish what kind of social rank his adversary holds and how it must be treated. If the negotiator intends to smother objections or heckling queries, then he should make his presentation a rapid-fire, hammer-and-tongs affair, protecting himself against interruption by a thick-skinned assurance.

He can stymie the adversary's attempts at delay, postponement and diversion. From his own experience, he can do what is necessary to prolong the adversary's attention span. On foreign soil, he must win dominance, hold it, and use it for a successful presentation. Side-show barkers can do this; so must he.

The core of presentation, whether through the exercise of a dominance technique or its converse, depends on getting a firm hand on the negotiating tiller from the outset. A lone negotiator capitalizes his personality, bringing into play attractive peculiarities of speech and phrasing that, even though interpretation into the foreign tongue, magnetize his adversary. When several negotiators work together as a team they can alternate their attributes. One of them can make the presentation tough; the other, more conciliatory, can give it a softer tone. This version of the police 'good guy — bad guy' operation makes up a useful pattern when practised abroad. Foreigners, although not ingenuous, accept the deceptive 'split' as offering an occasion for compromise. But neither the hard nor the soft approaches are ends in themselves. They serve their ends which converge on fixing attention on the presentation substance, the business in hand. When the presentation stage is complete, the foreign adversary's attention is total — and, in nine cases out of ten, he is led to believe that at least there are sensible talking points to be dwelt on, considered in a cooperative vein, and eventually agreed. It is impossible to lay out an infallible negotiating opening that will work wonders everywhere. Let it be enough to say that experienced negotiators can sense how best to get the centre of the conference stage.

Sometimes it is either the hard or the soft presentation. Sometimes it is a combination of elements taken from both. Sometimes it is a solicitous paternal 'this is the best for you' air that wins the adversary over from hostility to neutrality, which, after all, is at least half the battle. Perhaps this may be put into a nutshell by saying that the negotiator must demonstrate an ability to lead the business conferences abroad, to take his adversary along the road to agreement. In order to reach this agreement stage, the negotiator's presentation must fascinate the adversary's mind and excite his emotional responses. Admittedly this is a delicate job in one's own language, whether one's own cultural jurisdiction. In a strange country, speaking through an interpreter, the task is more difficult. All the more reason why the presentation should be prepared, equipped and demonstrated with as much expertise and care as time, place and circumstances abroad will permit. Pragmatically understood, the presentation is meant to get the customer's eyes and ears focussed on the negotiator first, then on what he has to offer, and finally on how he will wrap up the offer. If the presentation achieves all this abroad, the job is well done.

Time, place and circumstance

Luck is a transcendental ingredient of every international deal and so far as luck may be pinpointed, it consists of knowing how to be the right man at the right place at the right time. Some negotiators defy the fates and insist on going to the foreign country during a furious political upheaval. Others disregard national holidays, local religious festivals, weekends when no-one is in town, summer heat waves and transportation breakdowns. Banking on ill-deserved luck, they will hunt up thier quarry, beard him in his retreat, impose on his hospitality, and drag him protesting into the middle of a conference for which he has no desire, concerning some business to which he is presently opposed. Even worse, some negotiators make the journey without knowing exactly who the man is whom they ought to present themselves and their company's proposals. Why they obstinately do this is inexplicable, save on the theory that somewhere in their blood lines exist traces of primordial contacts with lemmings. How much easier, and more sensible it is for the negotiator to respect the foreign limitations on time, place and circumstance, and thus ensure a courteous welcome, however formal? In its place, they lay themselves open to a cold shoulder, and the very kind of hostility that can only impede their mission. Whatever favourable reception they had hoped for is doomed. What persuasive presentation they had hoped to produce will not be heard with an open ear, seen with an unprejudiced eye, or judged by an open mind.

Such negotiators must learn things the hard way. They are as much strangers to common sense as they are to good manners. Their disregard of decent and civil behaviour earns them nothing but disfavour. Their literal surprise visit, unheralded, unsponsored, and unsupported by the least comprehension of the local culture and convenience, can only bar their first attempts and mar their later ones. International negotiation, for them, is not their vocation. How they chose it must remain a secret.

International negotiation, like every other applied skill, demands attention to detail; the execution of detail separates the first-class negotiator from the others. With adequate care devoted to the details of presentation, the negotiator can expect the broad sweep of his business to take its course smoothly. On the other hand, if he omits the details, or performs them in a slovenly fashion, he jeopardises the hopes he held for straightforward progress from start to finish. This is particularly true of the time selection for his foreign conference. It cannot be stated too often, that time is critical to the success of the negotiation. 'Time' means foreign time, rather than the negotiator's habitual time. Spanish dinners at ten o'clock, American pre-breakfast conferences, English tea, Russian midnight sessions, Italian midday respites must be governed by local habits.

Obviously, emergencies and special situations may warrant, if not entirely excuse, abrupt appearances without prior notice. The better practice is to agree a time with the foreign side; and if this cannot be done conveniently, then the negotiator must think of local custom and shape himself to its time. If he has no choice but to seize the first moment and plunge ahead, he should try to soften the intrusion by some graceful act. The right sort of door-opening can spell the difference between an ultimate 'yes' and 'no'. No one enjoys being surprised, caught off-guard, in a negotiating state of undress — least of all foreigners who place much store in ceremony and even more in their disinclination to be hurried into immediate decision.

The negotiator's endeavour to meet the time requirements abroad should include a patient examination of air and rail and local travel schedules; and with them he should know what accommodations are at his disposal. Going to Milan in April without having made a hotel booking will find him right in the midst of a trade fair, with hardly a room open. Going to Teheran with a view toward meeting a government official will almost literally find him pitching a tent on the outskirts of that city unless he has made adequate arrangements for room and food long in advance of his arrival there. Similarly, it is necessary to scout out the mechanics of his arrival in whatever manner they will act on the conduct of his presentation. He ought to remember that 'packaging' his presence and his proposals simply means paying attention to details — of which time is the most important. there is no point in going to see the right man at the right place at the wrong time.

Tempo

Chess, tennis, fencing, acting, advocacy, dancing, courtship and international negotiation are subject to tempo. In spite of whatever a dictionary may say tempo is in great measure instinctual. At some moment in any of these activities, and in others, a current of control of assurance or continuity that favours us is felt. We know the feeling. We say that things are going right for us. Sometimes we can produce tempo not only once during an exchange but repetitively. Sometimes we know exactly what to do to gain a tempo. More often tempo is largely imperceptible in itself. Like a filterable virus we detect its operative nature through its effects. Granting that international negotiation is an art, creating a tempo is imprecise. But not entirely — although it is plastic and impermanent, on analyzing what we did to attain it, or what happened to cause us to lose it, we can form a fair judgment of its essentials. Admittedly, the style of gaining a tempo varies with the negotiator. Overall tempo can be tied into his style with sufficient certainty so that he can duplicate the essentials. Thus, by using a pause, by plucking at an ear-lobe, by dangling one's eyeglasses, by smiling, by altering the speed of speech, by rising from a chair and walking about, by staring into space, by a thousand and one apparently aimless but well calculated changes in how the negotiator chooses to appear, tempo can be won and held. Lawyers know this; salesmen (a species of advocate) know this; lecturers know this.

Tempo can be seen as a form of dominance. If there is a capture of tempo, the negotiator may be reasonably confident of imprisoning the attention of his foreign adversary. The difficulty, of course, rests in the fact that the adversary may be equally aware of the improtance of tempo and better skilled in establishing it in his own favour. A useful education in how to win tempo can be gotten in the theatre. Watch a polished performance of 'stage business'. See how innocuous fumblings with a coat button can rivet the audience's undivided attention. Notice how a small role takes on colour merely because the veteran ham inflects his voice in an unusual manner, or adds a comic turn to crossing the stage. When the juvenile comes through the french doors and with bright-eyed enthusiasm says 'Tennis anyone?' he gains, at least for that moment, tempo. The negotiator must know all about his capacity to capitalize on tempo; he should sudy himself. More than that, he should learn how to offset his adversary's attempts to disrupt him and steal tempo.

The principal function of tempo is simple: to aid the negotiator's presentation by providing continuity for what he intends to say or do. Subsidiary to this is the negotiator's need to counter-punch, to upset his foreign adversary's rebuttal, to disconcert his contradictions. Thus, for example, if the slow, painfully reasoned arguments of the other side require a methodical evolution, the negotiator should concentrate his efforts on conversational sniping. It need not be done rudely or obviously. In place of massing an enormous barrage of logical responses to be made at the close of the foreign adversary's remarks, he can interject 'Do you really believe that?' at the weak points of the remarks. The question can be enormously useful, for it searches the conscience of the adversary, challenges his veracity, disputes the realiability of what he says — and, of course, compels him to break off his tempo. If, as and when he does, the ngeotiator can pursue his advantage by saying something like this 'Now let me show you what I mean.' Then in full spate, he can take the bit of tempo in his teeth and leave the adversary far behind. Here too, as before, the negotiator may well suppose his adversary to know how to deal with such a situation. Indeed, if he knows something about the personality and character of the adversary, he will have prepared himself for such a possibility by saying 'Please let me finish.' Most often the adversary will stop dead in his tracks, forgetting that his tempo has been lost, that his was the argument that was disturbed, that the implication of impolite interruption attributable to himself is, to say the least, unfair. Tempo-control forms a most important part of the negotiator's persuasive techniques.

One thing should be said of tempo in foreign business conferences. The need for controlling it must be supplied within the local climate. What is acceptable by Russians (who are superb masters of the irrelevant interjection), would be only barely tolerable by Italians, and would be entirely rejected by the French. The English are impervious to interruptions. They sit tight and say 'Ah yes, but . . . '. And they go forward as doggedly as ever, somewhat resembling the launching of a lifeboat through a turbulent surf. It is the negotiator's duty to suit his tempo techniques to the custom of the country, the personality of his foreign adversary — and best of all, to his own style of elocution and 'stagecraft.' Finally, remembering that for the most part the interpreter will be the channel of communication, the negotiator ought to give his interpreter a rundown on how to communicate his tempo-control measures.

Disorientation and reorganization

International negotiation concerns an economic requirement that cannot be met at home. Whatever its substance and form, it must look abroad. When it does so, and succeeds in locating the desideratum, then the negotiating mechanism acts to match qualitative conditions to those determining terms of payment. Where the conditions and terms are standard, no issue of disorientation arises; and in its absense there is no need for reorganization.

The case is otherwise when extraordinary terms or conditions, or both, intervene in the foreign business. So, for instance, where the home company and the foreign company originally agree on conventional terms of payment, but cannot reduce them to contract because of newly imposed currency regulations, their tentative relationship becomes disoriented. By replacing the payment provisos with a triangulation, calling upon the paying party for commodities as adequate consideration for the foreign goods, the transaction will be reorganized. And if the commodities themselves are not to be tendered, but to be liquidated first and their proceeds are to be paid over to the foreign company, then the reorganization becomes a little more complex. Further, if the commodities are to be liquidated at some place other than one controlled by the immediate parties, the transaction assumes an even greater complexity, attended by even greater reorganization.

What reorganization signifies in this part of the discussion is a methodical accommodation by the transacting parties aimed at maintaining their contractual relationship in the face of external adverse forces. It might be stated more simply as a situation calling for a counter-offer with regard to terms and conditions that will effectuate the overall agreement. However, the distinctive character of this transaction is that the parties' original expectations were frustrated by the new legislation.

The eventual contract emerged from the parties' bilateral acceptance of disorientation. Nevertheless, at the outset, one of the parties must have had to persuade the other to accept a transaction different from that originally intended. Obviously, it was the party that needed the foreign materials, whose original agreed payment was interdicted by government, who had to convince the seller to accept the triangulation.

Here, the home company is the buyer, and the foreign one is the seller. The negotiator followed the problem to its source, namely: the foreign requirement for payment. But this placed the parties in opposition to each other. So he hit upon the idea of a 'no fault' discussion, the object of which was to draw the foreign adversary to his side as an ally facing the currency regulation threat to their community of interest in the success of the transaction.

In other words, he disoriented his adversary's innate hostility (under the conflict concept), and reorganized him into a friendly participant. This led to the next step, which, of course, was a natural development. The issue then became one of finding a substitute for currency as payment. Once the idea of substitution was agreed as furthering the transaction, several alternatives were considered, each of them containing probable advantages depending on the determination of 'complexity'. That is to say, the negotiator's offer of the triangulation itself would burden the seller with liquidating the commodity, assuming the market risks as well as those of transportation and storage. If the purchaser were to take over the liquidation, then the seller would have to abide the event of sale and wait for payment; and if the sale were to be conducted by some third party the risks pertinent to that event had to be thought over. The ultimate solution balanced the equities satisfactorily by providing adequate insurance coverage. The particulars are of no moment; the great thing was that the negotiator's initial venture, speaking psychologically, was correct. He converted the traditional seller/buyer opposition into a virtual partnership by disorientation, and then reformed the nature of the transaction in terms and conditions that advanced their common interests.

The recent example of the Ford Motor Company's similar technique is a case in point. It worked out a deal with Argentina for the sale of passenger automobiles against payment to be made by a quantity of sheep's wool seat covers, the value of which was set by an independent quantity surveyor in Cordoba (Argentina). On his report, each party undertook to make delivery, respectively, of the automobiles and covers.

Other forms of disorientation are related to fluctuation in market price. Thus where, in place of the conventional letter of credit, a Brazilian company offered 2,000 tons of coffee as payment against 1,000 tons of cold-rolled steel; the transaction was hinged to the market, so that a rise in steel would be met by an increased quantity of coffee, and vice versa.

Personality problems

Cultural differences influence personality disagreements between the negotiator and his foreign adversary. Whether the disagreements stem from the territorial imperative, the conflict concept, or endemic xenophobia, or the universal competition for a dominating position in the transaction, it is certain that they find expression in personality problems.

It would be unusual if this were not so when one takes into account the additional obstacles offered by doing business in at atmosphere charged with tension, where each side is trying to get the most and give the least, and where the communicating medium is an interpreter. The negotiator ought to overcome the impact of personality problems by assuming a conciliatory stance. So far as practicable, he should sidestep the occasions for quarrel, avoid giving provocation, and still maintain himself as the leader of the bargaining sessions.

Nothing should interfere with the substantive aims of the transaction. Everything should encourage its progress. Indulging in personal recrimination is not only unprofitable, it is unnecessary. Moreover, it may be taking on more than the negotiator can handle. And if it leads to an exchange of endless filibustering, the success derived from a petty personal triumph cannot balance the loss of the transaction and the company's investment in going abroad.

Keeping a cool head, avoiding gratuitous abrasions, eschewing denigratory remarks may be difficult, but it is more sensible than aspersing the foreign adversary's political philosophy, decrying his obtuseness, and ridiculing his mannerisms or professional competence. Once the personality problems come to the surface, they diminish any transactional success. This, perhaps, illustrates the uses of formal diplomatic language. A restrained, if sterile, vocabulary can dissipate angry outbursts. Unless the negotiator can accept the need for an unruffled demeanor, he should pack his bags, pull up stakes, close trails and go home. For his tactics will be at cross purposes with his company's international policy. Exceptions exist where it is necessary to appear to lose patience, to simulate anger, to act disappointed, to give the impression of outraged dignity. But, apart from the exceptional cases, the negotiator should be capable of maintaining what the Italians call *una buona figura.* So long as he can put a good face toward his adversary, the deal will inch ahead, despite the controversial personalities. He may even win his adversary to friendliness, which is not a small thing.

Reality and fiction of hostility

Hostility is a cultural fact to be expected, dealt with and mastered by the negotiator. As traders, or even as visitors, when we go abroad we excite wariness and fear because we are strange, what we do is strange, and how we show ourselves is strange. But this has always been so. We react the same way to those who enter our territories. Xenophobia is as old as the hills, or at least as old as the people who first inhabited them.

There are two kinds of xenophobia. The first fastens on aliens as stereotypes; this is associative revulsion. The second, selective, is exhibited because of our personalities. Thus, ethnicity is the key to associative xenophobia, and individually unacceptable characteristics to selective xenophobia. Foreigners are unwelcome; perhaps the degree of hostility is tempered by time, accommodation and acculturation. Nevertheless, no matter how worldly we are, we fear the unknown; and when we go to a foreign country we should see the fear as real. Stereotypes are broad, inaccurate, and therefore unreliable. Americans are coarse, crass, immature, superficial, inventive, and unpleasant. Englishmen are aloof, class-conscious, reticent, deceitful, and unpleasant. Italians, from the north, are romantic, artistic, inconstant, gay and tyrannical; from the south, they are sly, vengeful, avaricious, brutal, superstitious, and unpleasant. Germans are pedantic, arrogant, insufferable, maudlin, industrious, musical, and unpleasant. The French are gay, bright, lyrical, egoistic, insincere, greedy, arrogant and unpleasant. Spaniards are proud, cruel, handsome, and unpleasant. Hungarians are charming, chivalrous, inconsequential and stupid. Russians are primitive, loud, secretive, indomitable, enchanting, thick-headed, virtuous, openhanded and unpleasant. So it goes; stereotypes say everything, and nothing. Every traveller confirms by his presence his national stereotype — or modifies it for better or worse. When he leaves, the natives will say 'This Guarnarian is not half-bad; he's something like us'. Or, 'This Guarnarian is just like the others, only worse'. This leaves the negotiator with the need to make himself a living, moving, sentient contradiction of his stereotype. That's the place of beginning for all his foreign business and psychological techniques of persuasion. The stereotype, as bad as it is, gives him plenty of scope to make a useful personal impact. And in doing so, he can only improve the stereotype, making it easier for him to return for future business abroad.

Generally, all varieties of xenophobia, real or fancied, can be quieted by the personal behaviour of the negotiator. His conduct can dispel the unfavourable elements of the stereotype. If the xenophobic antipathy is selective, then he has only himself to blame. In democratic countries, it is easier for him to make his individuality an antidote to whatever stereotypical handicap attaches to him. In authoritarian countries, it is difficult to do so because of the rigid doctrinal control. In many countries the stereotype is fictive and may be disregarded. Thus, in the third world areas, nationality as such is less important than political affiliation, and since political movements are mercurial, volatile and unpredictable, the negotiator has a stronger footing for his presence and purpose.

One way to overcome any form of xenophobia is to demonstrate the benefits of the transaction as they will accrue to the community; establishing community interest with the foreign company is easier when the interest in the community speaks for itself through the negotiations. Here are a dozen advantages that may attach wholly or partially to an international transaction:

Area	Benefit
1 *Labour*	Increased employment, increased per capita disposable income
2 *Municipal development*	Exploitation of local resources
3 *Cash flow*	Increased volume of trade, turnover, encouragement for new enterprise
4 *Industrial center*	Attractive to other heavy and light manufacturing and assembly plants
5 *Land values*	Industrial and commercial intensification increases land values
6 *Housing and transportation*	New enterprise needs new labour, new homes and transit facilities

7 *Social service*	Increased industry, commerce and employment provide higher tax returns, reduce local costs for social welfare, eliminate unemployability
8 *Law and order*	Increased standard of living and opportunity to satisfy human needs by direct employment and social services reduce crime caused by economic factors
9 *Cultural integration*	Coordinated industrial, commercial and financial resources promote growth and expanding economic sufficiency
10 *Government participation*	Economic improvement with municipal sponsorship and government support attracts outside capital investment and promotes local funding for community
11 *Government contracts*	Economic expansion at local level attracts grants, subsidies, tax exemptions for establishment of plants operating under government contracts
12 *Political prestige*	Expanding local economy and social activities increase political power, influence and representation on national and regional levels

The negotiator, in addition, to the natural results expected from his transaction with the foreign country, can enhance its appeal by emphasizing the foregoing community spinoffs, any of which are self-explanatory community inducements. In such examples, or others he might be able to demonstrate as attributable to the transaction, he will find ample grounds on which to rest his local version of 'what is good for General Motors is good for the country'. From a practical view, since most international business must appeal to the foreign government for licenses, approvals and certifications essential to establishment and operation, the fact that the local community will draw derivative economic and social advantages from the enterprise can be a critical force in swaying the foreign adversary to accept the contractual relationship.

Finally, apart from the community's improvement, it is plain that the foreign adversary's personal prestige will benefit from his initiative in introducing the home company's resources and directives to the local scene. His own political standing, not to mention the opportunities for political preferment, will rise with the success of the transaction. Indeed, there is every reasonable prospect that all of the latent and patent hostility ordinarily massed in opposing such a transaction will be stilled by the community's appreciation of the advantages to be obtained under the forthcoming contract.

This interworking of community interest and private anticipations on whatever scale is appropriate to the negotiation should be kept in sight. By linking them together, the negotiator and his foreign adversary convert the community to acquiescence, allay suspicion, abate opposition, and supply all of the local officials with a pragmatic proof of the proposition that 'one hand washes the other'.

Even if local conditions cannot be immediately advanced, the intention to do so exhibits the negotiator's good will. From the classic principles of behavioural control, he is seen as stimulating affirmative motivation through incentives and rewards that are unimpeachable. In light of what was earlier stated with reference to bribery and corruption, how much easier it is to provide morally acceptable justifications:

Working within the range of possibility

The negotiator must always limit himself to what 'is in the cards'; that is to say, his terms and conditions, and those proposed to him, must lie in what can be established as a factual circumstance; or, alternatively, it must be foreseeable. To count on circumstances that are obviously impossible to predict destroys credibility, and, worse, encourages the other side to make unreliable and exaggerated commitments that, in the long run, are counter productive.

In this sense, foreign negotiations must be weighed against existing market forces first of all. Then, external factors must be evaluated. These, generally speaking, are constant or variable. The former lend themselves to predictability; the latter do not. However variables may possess a certain incidence that can be measured within acceptable limits; and if they can be foreseen within those limits, the calculations gain a quantum of regularity. For example, with reference to variables, it is possible to correlate the effect of an increase in the American prime rate of interest to the exchange rate of English pound sterling, even though it may not be possible to forecast precisely when the prime rate will rise or fall. So, in a US/UK negotiation a British plant owner's purchase of American machine tools must reasonably look ahead to the cost of financing the purchase by borrowing. The repayment of principal and interest on the loan must be covered. One way to do so with some degree of certainty is to mention that the payment will amortize the principal and interest, with the rate of interest fixed as of the date of contract; this affords a hedge against any subsequent rise in the prime rate. It may also open the way for the English purchase to borrow, so to speak, from the American manufacturer; the loan form may follow a delayed payment scheme under which the time of repayment provided is extended as an equivalent for the money factor.

Variables, logically, create uncertainty. However, they cannot be excluded from the course of commerce. What can be done is to work around them by providing contractual alternatives that lie within the range of possiblity. So, the preceding illustration permits the variable factor to be considered within the range by limiting its operative effect; and this is done by using the delayed payment scheme.

Apart from such devices that permit containment of variables, the negotiator must be alert to proposals that are precatory rather than pragmatic. They rest on unjustifiable hope. They cannot be supported by arithmetic, logic or even divination. Yet even here, in special instances, some sort of solution can be worked out by procuring protective insurance. In this day and age, insurance seems to be available as required. The risk factors are set by the insurance carrier; the premium is determined with respect to the risk. If the negotiator's company wants the transaction badly enough, it can hedge against the impossibility; or, putting it the other way, it can insure itself against the risk by paying the going price for the premium. This makes sense. However, it does not release the negotiator from his duty to watch out for promises that cannot be performed. It is up to him to keep his company's commitments within the range of what it can do; and, at the same time, he must not take for granted that his foreign adversary's company can or will do all it agrees under the contract.

It is futile to commit his company to an all requirements contract that it is not physically equipped to perform. Even the expectation that it might sub-contract its obligations is not enough to warrant the commitment, except when the foreign company is appraised of the situation, approves the proposed subcontracting, and accepts the risks inherent in the agreement. It may be argued that all commercial contracts are fraught with risk, and that it is impossible to eliminate risk. True enough, but the position does not turn on the presence of risk, rather it is concerned with the nature of what can be done in the range of possibility. Assumed risks possess a character quite different from commitments to what cannot fall within the foreseeable range of possibility.

This raises the question of whether the ngeotiator has the authority to halt the international negotiation if his on-the-spot judgment tells him that the foreign company is not now capable of carrying out the commitment on its part. To answer the question we have to know what the negotiator's specific authority is. It varies from case to case. As an example, if he has been told to negotiate for an oil lease, this does not of itself imply that he must have proof positive of the existence of an oil pool on the land. The responsibility for that item is with his company. However, if his instructions are subject to his receipt of proof positive that oil pools do exist, then he cannot continue the negotiation toward contract in the absence of that proof. To do so would place the transaction beyond the range of foreseeable possibility. It would also be a breach of faith and responsibility on his part, not to mention a total disregard of his duty as a negotiator.

Rites, ceremonies and mutual respect

Contract-making is solemn in its inception because the rights and obligations to which it gives form are intended to be punctiliously marked, privately honoured and publicly performed, or, on default enforced. They are hallowed by custom and usage, regulated by law, and invested with the sanction of tradition, morality and communal interest. That contracts are breached, evaded and flouted does not diminish, but rather increases, the need for their ceremonial execution.

Abroad, as at home, contracts must be valid when entered into and valid when the provisions are questioned. To this end, the rites attendant on their formation, the ceremonies accompanying their execution, and the respect given to their substance are entitled to observance; for they supplant the fallibility of human memory, and in so doing enjoy the deference within the territorial limits of the state wherein they bind the contracting parties,

For this reason the negotiator must be zealous in following the local prescriptions refereable to his transaction. His duty to his company does not allow him to treat a contract carelessly. While he need not be a lawyer, or, indeed even if he is one, the consequences in law should be plain to him as they are to the highest tribunal at the place where agreement is set down. Should the negotiator be in doubt as to the terms and conditions of the contract, or how they will be construed, he should suspend the execution of the written instrument until his doubt is resolved. It is useless to sign first and determine later what meaning will be attached to the contract. That this, unfortunately, is frequently done does not negate the need to ensure the conformity of the contract with what the local law explicitly requires. It is not a mark of sophistication to say 'Of course I'll sign it and give it over to our legal department for their opinion'.

A blithe disregard for the formalities of contract-making may lead his company into loss, damage and penalty. At best, it brings them to the verge of litigation which destroys the very relationship sought by the negotiation. Forgetting to dot the 'i's' and cross the 't's' is human, but costly. Allowing the foreign adversary to do so is an unforgiveable error. Insistence on compliance with the formalities is plain common sense. And when the adversary says 'Don't you trust us?', that is the time to persist in absolute regularity and thus safeguard his company against a subsequent pretext that the contract is void for non-compliance with the rites and ceremonies.

As to 'respecting' the contract after it has been executed, the matter lies within the discretion of the parties, that is to say the domestic and the foreign companies. It is possible to waive the strict performance provided for in the contract without nullifying its sense and substance. A clause may later appear unfeasible for reasons and circumstances not earlier contemplated. As an example, if the domestic company has agreed to take delivery of a cargo of wheat arriving by the *S.S. Argo* at Port Everglades, and the vessel has been re-routed because of a dock strike, the parties may do the sensible thing and make mutual adjustments to suit the circumstance. If the contract calls for notices of damage to be filed within twenty days after delivery to destination and the merchandise is found defective on the tenth day, but communication facilities are disrupted because of civil disturbance, adjustments can be made amicably. And the contract will be respected in its essence. 'Respecting' the contract implies a willingness to act in accordance with its provisions coupled with the performance of such acts as were intended to run between the principals. This cannot include, for example, bad faith performance, no matter how many written protestations of good faith are sent by the defaulting party to the other.

While the negotiator has no responsibility for the events that ensure upon the execution of the contract, he does bear the burden of instilling his foreign adversary with a lively regard for the contract. And the best way to accomplish this, and thus discharge the burden, is to see to it, under advice of counsel, that the contract incorporates as many avenues of relief and recoupment as are legally available. Sometimes his foreign adversary will say that they are unnecessary technicalities, that it never has been his (the foreign) company's policy to subscribe such technical provisions, that his company has always faithfully performed its obligations. All the more reason to suggest that there is always a first time. If his insistence is reasonable, and the foreseen defaults are within general commercial experience, or, indeed, if they can arise because of circumstances peculiar to the transaction or the novel position of the parties, then the negotiator can do no less than explain his reasons and hammer home his demand for the inclusion of the provisions. his single alternative is to take the opinion of company counsel. Very often, thousands of miles away from legal advice, this may be impractical. He then should seek local counsel, consult with him, and exercise his discretion as to how far he may omit protection.

Chapter 8

How to reach agreement

Framing objectives, narrowing issues, discovering and isolating differences, philosophical barriers, accepting and rejecting non-negotiability, strategy, tactics, techniques, style and flair.

Framing objectives

Purpose and objective are frequently used interchangeably. In this discussion, purpose signifies the totality of the aims of the foreign business. It is, in this sense, a synonym for the overall strategy. Objective is a strategic element. Thus, the purpose of a negotiation by Volkswagen in the United States is to set up an assembly plant. One of the objectives in doing so is to gain an insight into American technology. Adding the objectives of VW together gives us its overall purpose. Purpose usually is rigid; objectives may vary with the course of the transaction. So, where the purpose is to export steel, the objectives may originally focus on establishing a local agent; further consideration may suggest outright sale to a foreign purchaser. The strategy then will be shaped in accordance with the modification; offers may go out via trade papers, to be followed by sending the negotiator abroad to make personal contact with intending purchasers, eliminating the need to pay commissions to the local agent.

The flexibility of the objective is essential, so that the transaction can be preserved by whatever accommodations are indicated by opportunity in the foreign market. In other words, company policy, once agreed, can be steered through the vicissitudes of special events that touch the balance between supply and demand; stated even more simply, if the cat must be skinned, then there are many ways to do it. Any of these ways, according to the needs of the moment, is an objective.

Within the context of these comments, we can see the implications of the phrase 'keeping one's options open', which is sound thinking by management. How far the negotiator may be at liberty to switch options, or objectives, while in the mid-stream of a foreign negotiation is debatable. It is easier said than done when one is on top of the bargaining. Be that as it may, there can be no doubt that policy lies in the province of management, that the purpose of the negotition is set by management, and that its objectives fall within the scope of that purpose. In real-life situations, when the negotiator faces a need for a changed objective, he usually calls time out for further instructions from the home office.

The correct framing of objectives, together with such restatements as are required in the spirit of negotiating 'give and take', is tactically sound because it appears logical and is logical in presenting afirmative avenues to contract. In doing so, it takes the foreign adversary away from negative responses. He cannot just say 'No'. He is placed squarely on the debating firing line; and in order to justify his negation, if he can, he will reveal himself far more than he would have done otherwise. Should he actually be using the negotiation a a cover for some ulterior reason, the conciliatory alternatives will smoke him out. Either he will accept one of them, or be forced into a flat refusal to bargain further. So far as tactics are related to the objectives, the negotiator can present the alternatives right from the beginning, maintaining a 'dead pan' expression, and giving his foreign adversary all the leeway to make his selection from the lot. This tactic preserves the negotiator's dominance, continues his control of tempo, and feints the adversary into accepting the objectives sought, no matter which alternative is agreed.

The presentation of framed objectives, once again for tactical reasons, should not be made in a discernible order of importance, so to speak. The negotiator can shuffle them about, very much like the card expert who invites the reader to 'pick a card, any card in the pack'.

The negotiator ought never to expose himself to the employment of the same tactics against his position. Leaving options, alternatives and objectives to the moment of first encounter is risky. Improvization cannot match preparation. Even a brilliant invention at the last moment comes off badly by comparison when we take into account that by the time the last-minute brainchild is examined in the cool light of practicality, it will stir up more trouble than a hornet's nest, especially with regard to ministerial matters. The reason for this is that the negotiator working under pressure to complete the transaction at any cost may believe he has introduced the precise element when, in fact, there are many considerations working against its practical operation. And, in the heat of the exchanges made hurriedly, these considerations are overlooked or inadequately accounted for. In short, well-framed objectives, fleshed out by a quiver of alternatives provide flexibility, bargaining control and negotiating grace, all without unnecessary risk or concession.

The best-framed objectives are flexible, affording ample scope for restatement of offers and counteroffers. When objections are raised by the other side, the negotiator should be able to rephrase the proposal, retaining the substance of the objective, while tendering a more acceptable form. Sometimes this flexibility can serve two uses. First, it allows the negotiator to eliminate the cause of controversy by a substitution of less offensive language. Second, it provides the means for giving the foreign adversary 'something to take back' to the foreign company. If, for example, he can establish him self as 'winning' a change in the negotiations, his face is saved, and his company position will be preserved. No-one likes leaving a negotiation empty-handed. This is particularly true in transactions where the domestic company holds all of the negotiating cards and is virtually able to dictate the terms on which the contract will close.

Again, where both sides are equally well situated in bargaining strength, the negotiator's apparent willingness to draw the objectives in a different light can only demonstrate his inclination toward conciliation, and thus attract a like response from the adversary. The ability of both sides to objectify their bargaining through patient restatements can only expedite eventual agreement. For each side can guard against being boxed in by ambiguities or uncertainties in language. And, in addition, the spirit of amicable negotiation-in-language protects the transaction against unfortunate personal intransigence.

Having in mind the benefits to gained from flexibility, the negotiator can prepare himself for the foreign criticism by posing questions such as 'If I suggest this statement in these words, how will he (the foreign adversary) react?'. 'If I then present him with these alternative statements, which of them would be more acceptable to him?' Having hypothesized the likelihood of objection and reformation, the negotiator can go farther in his preparation by anticipating the need for logically supporting the alternative statements; and this can be done through tying them to a reasoned opinion, citing whatever authority is suitable and available. The value of doing this apart from the obvious benefits, is that the foreign adversary is deprived of the opportunity of making wholly specious arguments. He must face the substance of the proposals, and in doing so he will reveal whether or not his negotiating intentions are serious and sincere.

Narrowing the issues

The best way to deal with this tactic is to imagine a number of situations which, however different from each other, are alike in one respect: they employ an aggressive manoeuvre designed to constrict the free movement of the defender. However they manage this tactic, it always limits the area of the opponent. The limitation extends to what movements are available, and the space within which they may be exercised. A boxer, and a fencer, for example, always understand the importance not only of limiting available space and the movements within it, but also of being able to concentrate his own offensives more effectually as a result of the tactics. Tennis players are adept at cutting their opponent's court down by driving him to the side-lines, and then angling their shots to the far side which is exposed and incapable of defense. Formal logic uses major and minor premises to the same effect. Once the other side is narrowly confined by accepting the premises, his intellectual operations cannot take him safely home. The progression toward conclusion is inevitable.

International negotiations should be looked at with the same tactical appreciation. Not all issues are equally urgent, or valid, or even arguable. It would be wasteful in many ways for the negotiator to bedevil himself with extraneous matter, unless, of course, to do so suits his purposes. However, it is rare that he will have the time to spend on dilatory pursuits. In the ordinary negotiation abroad, he will want to get to the heart of the transaction as quickly and efficaciously as possible. And one of the best ways to this end is through what we call a narrowing of issues. This tactic requires him to sort out, classify and arrange the quesions to be resolved. Thus, inspection of an oil storage tank is an important issue; in the absence of special circumstances, the precise hour of inspection is not an important issue. The negotiator should focus on agreeing the inspection, and concentrate his fire on that issue, not principle issue must be determined before the negotiator goes abroad. It may be suggested that although he knows, or should know, what is 'principal' to his company, he cannot know how the other side will determine the issues. This is logically true, but in a practical sense, in most negotiations the germane, important and debatable issues can be separated from the others with a fair certainty that both sides will hold the same opinion of them, at least as to their strategic importance.

This being so, why then must the negotiator look to the matter of narrowing the issues? The answer is that his purpose abroad must be attended to in specific time period. The other side knows this. If they can derail his attention to non-productive, trivial and collateral issues, he will have consumed his time, exhausted his patience, and locked himself into a situation which requires him to leave the conference without satisfying his instructions or, at best, reaching only some of his objectives — and these under pressure to get aboard the last return flight. A good part of the art of negotiation hangs on the technique of radiating calmness, giving the appearance of unhurried leisure within which to weigh the plus and minus values of each relevant proposal. The technique will be frustrated, if the other side gets the negotiator to spend his energy and waste his ammunition on inconsequentialities.

Formally, a straight-line approach to the business discussions can be made by means of a prepared agenda. And in order to forestall subsequent filibustering, it is useful to procure the adversary's agreement to the agenda, preferably in writing. Then, assuming that both sides now know and respect each other's expertise, they can screen out the minnows and deal with the big negotiating fish. Doing so precludes forensic fireworks, displays of personal umbrage accompanied by 'This point may not be important to you, but it is to me. Do you dare to challenge my good faith?'

Temperamental exhibitions should be regarded for what they are. In failing to reduce their incidence, the negotiator is surrendering to his foreign adversary all of the advantages of dominance, tempo control, and time-running-against-the-clock. Furthermore, he is exposing himself to picayune sniping, delaying devices and diversions. Once the adversary succeeds in converting the contractual issues into dramatic free-for-all, the negotiator has no recourse save to sit tight and put up with the theatricalisms.

There are naturally such occasions that constitute exceptions, such as the intervention of new circumstances that raise new and grave issues. Thus the bankruptcy of a subcontractor, the take-over of a competitor, the loss of a friendly government contact, all must be dealt with from scratch. Such issues should be treated as major ones, and allowance for their discussion must be made in the negotiating time-table. This is only right and sensible, and international negotiators have sufficient experience in mutual accommodation to take up new issues.

Discovering and isolating differences

Because the success of the foreign business requires agreement, and agreement depends on harmonizing differences, it is necessary for the negotiator to discover them as early as he can, preferably even before he goes abroad. The principal sources of difference lie in culture and language. As to language, either he will command a sufficient fluency so that communications between him and his foreign adversary will pass muster, or, as is common, he will have the assistance of an interpreter to ensure that they do. Culture presents a problem that is at once deceptive and difficult to appreciate for its relevance. As has been noted earlier, it bears directly on every aspect of the negotiation and conditions the communications themselves, the adversary's attitudes and responses, and, most of all, the meeting of the minds that is fundamental to final agreement.

Culture comprises the sum of the foreignness which the negotiator must deal with. It takes in the physical environment, the history, the traditions, the activities, the social structures, the ordering of government, the spirit and the philosophy prevalent in the foreign country. The ethnic characteristics of the people, their habitual movements and their material expectations as well as their religious practices all come together at the negotiation in the person of the foreign adversary. For the negotiator to be competent he should be conversant with the foreign culture; he must look out for and discover the differences it represents; and he must isolate them. By 'isolate', we mean to say that he must give them an evaluation that will enable him to accept them as facts that influence his adversary, not as predispositions toward ill-will.

At the negotiation, in order to ascertain and discount these differences, the negotiator's preliminary conversations, even on minor topics will supply him with confirmation of what he previously suspected; or, on the other hand, he might find that his earlier impression of the local culture needs to be corrected. In either event, whatever he learns will be extremely helpful in choosing his approaches, applying his persuasive techniques and effectuating his negotiating tactics.

Occasionally, his reconnaissance into the personality of his adversary will illuminate the nature of the opposition as a pro forma gesture, made as part of the group pattern. Just as, in some foreign countries, there is a fixed courtship pattern between boy and girl, so there is a fixed negotiating pattern that compels the foreign adversary to sit in stony silence, shake his head and reject initial offers regardless of their content. Knowing the cultural differences, and isolating them, can make the difference between a communicating impasse and a freeway. If the negotiator takes the initiative in opening up the conversations, he can introduce a number of topics that will highlight the reactions across the table. The most useful ones are such as will lay the groundwork for mutuality. Where the cultures of the parties are parallel, almost any well-managed conversation will strike common ground somewhere during the exchange. Where they are far apart, the negotiator must work harder. The negotiator has nothing to lose, and in his efforts he has a right to count on a lucky breakthrough that can be exploited.

As an example, the writer and an English colleague took part in a negotiation with a Japanese paper manufacturer, intending to reach contract for the exportation of special paper products from Japan to England. The Englishman, an experienced negotiator and business man, at once opened a number of points of conversational attack. Imaginatively, and with a respectable interspersal of Japanese words and phrases, he spoke about

Japanese art, touching on wood-block prints, netsui pieces, and the Kabuki. He then went on to Japanese beer, whiskey and sake. He continued with the Japanese excellence in tennis, golf and industrial competition. The Japanese gentleman, about 80 years of age, said absolutely nothing. He smiled, vigorously nodded his head, and looked vaguely into the distance, where the geisha girls were hovering about. The writer noted the continued lack of contact and said to the Englishman 'Charles, your curves are missing the plate'. At this the Japanese gentleman sat up and proudly stated 'I pitch. I pitch smokeball forty years ago'. The conversation turned to the Brooklyn Dodgers, the New York Yankees and the various American teams that had played baseball in Japan. The ice was broken. And the Englishman skillfully took his opportunity and turned the conversation back to business. Trade terms were agreed in principle. The following day the terms and conditions of a profitable contract capped the negotiation, and the enterprise got off to a pleasant start.

One never can tell when abroad just what will trigger amity or incur enmity. Only a willingness to tap the cultural stream is needed to start the negotiating process. Sometimes, by pure chance, as we know, a topic will surface and lead to just the right occasion for pursuing the core of the business. Certain topics are traditionally unsafe even in one's own market at home. Politics, religion, phsyical idiosyncracies, extramarital relations and the immorality of competitors should be excluded as a matter of course. Here too, exceptions may exist abroad. Personal health, family foibles, business operations, hopes and dreams, even when tied to the tabu topics, are acceptable in Mid-Eastern negotiations, so long as they do not reflect adversely on the foreign adversary. He may relish them as they affect others, but such topics may cut too near to his bone to be enjoyed. In any case, it is in questionable taste to trifle with what may be offensive.

Strangely enough, 'isolating differences' responds to the stage-settings for the conference. Some negotiators quickly assess the first intimations of the psychological quotient of their adversaries and know, almost instinctively, when taking the head of the table will only strain the atmosphere with defensive or counter-aggressive ploys. So they see to it that a table, round or octagonal, suits the foreign adversary's ego; that it does not impel him to self-assertion; that it avoids the slightest hint of rudeness. And if the local negotiating customs require the adversary to have his secretary's 'secretly' take shorthand memos on a pad held beneath the table, there is no need to worry about that, or question it, or make a to-do about excluding the secretary. This, after all, does not affect the meat-and-potatoes considerations governing contract. And if the negotiator is anxious about preserving absolute secrecy while he is abroad, he should be well aware of the nearly impossible task of doing so, especially in authoritarian countries. All he needs do to appreciate the phrase, 'Even the walls have ears' and remember his home town, where behind every curtained window someone with nothing better to do would be sitting and making mental notes on every passerby, human or otherwise. The notes would be chewed over, talked over, enlarged beyond semblance to reality, and then from village mouth to village ear given currency and free rein, far beyond factual truth.

The whole point about discovering and isolating differences rests on the need for opening up the mental and emotional responses intelligently, so that the adversary's intentions and his company's ability to go to contract can be diagnosed accurately. Once the differences are sorted out and effectively done away with, then there is nothing standing in the way of reaching agreement. Overcoming the cultural road-block, fortification, barrier or however it may be designated is a tactical necessity to be met by the negotiator. He may choose to do so head-on or by leap-frogging, by meeting engagements, by flanking attacks. But he must succeed or else chalk up a zero.

Philosophical barriers

If we label cultural differences, we can perceive them and deal with them. But some cultural differences do not lend themselves to easy identification. One of them is the difference in philosophical outlook and judgment between us and 'them'. Although we may not possess a clearly defined personal philosophy, we have no hesitation in saying 'My philosophy is' thus and so. We believe we think systematically, and, above all, correctly. Therefore, although we recognize the possibility that other philosophies exist, we do not receive them on the same level. As an example, the Western economic philosophy supports the individual's right of self-determination as a theory.

In practice, the theory is hedged about by 'public interest' that is conceived as opposed to private interest. Abroad, in authoritarian nations, the only economic philosophy is that pronounced and practised by the State, and the individual, as part of the State, is identified with it. What this means is that a curious inversion takes place in the General Motors axiom. In the Eastern Bloc, what is good for the State is good for the State Agency is good for the individual, who, after all, is a molecular unit of the State.

As a consequence, any consideration of 'personal' philosophy by an Eastern Bloc negotiating adversary is contrary to the reality of the State, inimical to its safety, and a dangerous conversational gambit, one that only cause trouble to himself and to the negotiator who mistook a smile for an invitation to an old-fashioned bull session.

On another plane, in the Western commercial world, bankruptcy is a serious economic event, trailing all kinds of interventions (as by trustees, receivers, referees and so on) and penalties, such as loss of credit, compulsory submission to examinations, fines, loss of personal property, and even criminal penalties are imposed, with varying degrees of severity. This is part of the Western 'philosophy'. Elsewhere, bankruptcy is regarded otherwise, merely as a visitation from above in consequence of stupidity, or of excessive cupidity. The philosophical aspect tends to show bankruptcy as a logical proof of being 'unlucky', and the practical effect of the 'philosophy' is to let the insolvent try his luck again 'elsewhere's' philosophy is cynical and pragmatic. After all, if the bankrupt recoups he will be able to pay some portion of his debts. And if his recoupment is at the expense of others who know nothing of his commercial unsuccess and trust him, so much the worse for them.

The preceding rough generalization suffices to alert the Western negotiator to the need to check and double-check the creditworthiness of the foreign country, the character of his foreign adversary and the reputation for fair conduct both possess. He must recognise that the foreign company may be cooking up a scheme to acquire assets, goods, wares and merchandise for which payment will not be made; that the acquisitions will be concealed from creditors, sold out of the regular course of trade, and the proceeds used to line the pockets of the bankrupt and a few carefully chosen trade friends.

Cheating some creditors at the expense of others is not unknown abroad. Preferential treatment is common, difficult to punish, and time-consuming. Using dummy companies as screens for siphoning off assets and pocketing the proceeds is as common as sin.

The negotiator needs to get under the skin of his foreign adversary, find out his 'philosophy', and then determine whether that philosophy is a barrier to a reliable and profitable relationship with the negotiator's company. This cannot be done by taking a check-list to the conference table. A lot of spadework is necessary. Some of it will be accomplished by the domestic company's market surveys and background briefings on the foreign company's operational record and executives. A good deal depends on the negotiator's 'hunch', his intuitive capabilities, his talent for smelling out the something that is rotten in Nairobi. Experience and training, education and elbow rubbing with veteran negotiators come in handy in providing him with a fifth negotiating wheel. Sometimes the apparent facts fly in the face of 'hunch'; when they do, the negotiator should rely on 'hunch'. Everything within his negotiating purview, however miniscular, should be noticed and measured — and one of the chief subjects for his critical notice is the local philosophy. Conspiracies to defraud do not arise by spontaneous combustion; they rest on a philosophy that anything goes if you can get away with it. Bribery, extortion and generalized corruption, whether in London, Paris, Rome, Vienna, Ankara or other compass points, do not emerge as a case of economic measles; they are the symptoms of an underlying philosophy that every man has his price; and if a combination of bull-dozing, ungentle persuasion, arm-twisting and offers that cannot be refused must be brought into play, it is only because it fits in the local philosophical picture. Even *caveat emptor* is a kind of philosophical warrant for cheating. It tells the buyer to watch out; but it does not stop the seller from violating fair trade and good conscience. The rule is let him save himself who can, and the devil take the hindmost.

It is necessary to say at this point that the writer's intention to note the relevance of negotiating philosophy is not to be seen as a soap-box for delivering moral screeds. What should be plain is that the negotiator must know with whom he is dealing, from where he comes, and what he represents in order to do international business safely and advantageously. Nothing that has been written here says that the negotiator should shy away from entering any foreign business in general or any foreign market in particular. The main thing is to avoid being injured by innocence. Where the local philosophy supports a lax view toward criminal conduct, it is certain that business and business negotiators will be no better than they should be, as the old expression has it. Candidly, even in countries where the economic philosophy strictly denounces economic irregularity, private immorality, and transactional duplicity, there is every good reason to suppose that someone is cheating someone every day of the year, successfully. And, of course, for every one who does so there are a hundred who are clumsy and fail. But the negotiator's job is to save his company from the foreign successful criminal.

Apart from the wide-open opportunities for corner-cutting abroad, the negotiator must be careful that his foreign adversary's philosophy does not encourage him to blink his eyes at shaving the dice so that the odds favour his company unfairly. There are so many ways to commit fraud that it would be beyond the writer's ability to even list them without comment. Neither numerical nor alphabetical classifications would exhaust human ingenuity in circumventing the law or turning 'philosophy' to the disadvantage of the negotiator. His failure to defend himself and his company could only be regarded as an attractive incitement to the commission of misdeeds, the violation of trust, and the betrayal of the hospitality due the stranger within the foreign gates. In this context, it would be very much worth the while of the negotiator to take most particular note of the local 'philosophy' prevalent in those countries where his company is venturing. When he does so, he will probably want to think and rethink the implications of its currency regulations and tax laws. As a result, he will be better able to grasp the point of the foreign adversary's suggestion that the proposed transaction be reflected in two different types of books and records, one for the government — and one for the interested parties. It would be interesting to discuss the proposal philosophically, of course, somewhere beyond 'four walls'.

Accepting and rejecting non-negotiability

For this discussion, non-negotiability attaches to any subject of a transaction that either side refuses to include in the bargaining. Where the negotiator abroad is trying to buy a cargo of Jaffa oranges and the seller refuses to fix the rate of exchange limitations within which payment will be accepted, the negotiator can either withdraw or agree that the prevailing rate at date of delivery shall measure the payment he will make. Of course, non-negotiability can be mutually agreed. But if so, there is no problem left for the negotiator. The real question lies in how to deal with the foreign adversary who refuses to entertain issues because he takes the position, for whatever cause, that they are not within the transaction — or, if they are, then they will not be subject to modification by his company.

The alternative for the negotiator is simple. He can "take it or leave it". But if he takes it, so to speak, then he commits his company to terms running against their instructions to him. If he leaves it, then the transaction comes to a dead end. The best way to tackle this difficulty is use a back-door tactic. Keep the negotiation alive on all negotiable items, while reserving the stumbling-block issues. At a later period, if the conference continues on a reasonably cordial basis, it may be more feasible to renew the attempt to include the reserved issues. First of all, the issues may resolve themselves as collateral or minor points of principal terms; and they can be dealt with as a matter of course. Secondly, if they remain important the negotiator may suggest the intervention of a conciliator so that the transaction may go to completion. Thirdly, especially in an international situation, the market changes may reduce the need — or the claimed need — for non-negotiability, and thus enable both sides to reach a compromise on them.

Experienced negotiators are not daunted by claims of 'non-negotiability'. They know that it is important for their foreign adversaries to make a show of strength at the outset of the negotiation. Secondly, they know that 'non-negotiability' is a useful device for prying some additional advantage that the other side might not justify through straight across the table bargaining. At some lull in the conference, the foreign negotiator might drop a hint that he has reviewed the matter and would be disposed to withdraw 'non-negotiability' in exchange for a concession to be made by the negotiator. Occasionally 'non-negotiability' is raised because the foreign adversary does not have specific authority to negotiate on a particular issue. And not infrequently, he may raise the objection simply by reason of the fact that he has not enough information about its strategic importance to the overall transaction. There are, moreover, some foreign negotiators whose value judgments are defensive. So they stake out a 'non-negotiable' issue, whether in fact it is so is debatable, a line to which they can retreat if the other facets of the negotiation are going against them. Doing so permits them to say, 'this is not negotiable now; and since it is not, there is no point in going through the motions on the other items'. Finally, 'non-negotiability' is urged merely for the reason that the other side does not know how to take any position without injuring his company. In this last instance, the negotiator can use common sense and propose an examination of the probable result of including the issue in question. He can illustrate and detail the several alternatives. The foreign adversary, given a choice, in all likelihood revises his position and accepts one of the alternatives, providing it is fairly drawn.

Reversing the case, how should the negotiator raise 'non-negotiability' on behalf of his company? The best way to do so is to avoid formal declarations that are hard and fast. He loses nothing by saying 'I'm not sure that we ought to talk about this now', or 'I'd like to turn this about for a week or so', or 'Let's see how important this point is after we settle point X'. In other words, unless he intends to be obdurate, the use of 'non-negotiability' should not be blatant. After all, it is he who is travelling abroad. And it sounds awkward for him to say that he has come to negotiate, but will not negotiate item X, or whatever the subject matter might be.

There is nothing wrong, however, with withdrawing negotiability from an item if his adversary seems too ready to use 'non-negotiability' as a snag. At a later moment during the negotiations both sides can come to a trade-off on satisfactory terms, agreeing to withdraw 'non-negotiability'.

It is, obviously, easier to accept negotiable issues than non-negotiable ones. There always is the feeling that by accepting issues as non-negotiable, a bargaining edge is given away. However, the negotiator faces the possibility that if he rejects 'non-negotiability' out of hand, he has cut himself and his company off from further communication. As a suggestion, he might consider saying that 'for the time being, I agree to exclude item X — but without prejudice to my right to raise it later on'.

The statements does no harm, and keeps the bargaining alive.

Intelligence Checklist For Negotiating Strategy and Tactics In Foreign Markets

1 *Information used for management decision*
   a. Market surveys
   b. Feasibility studies
   c. Miscellaneous reports
   d. Evaluations and assessments
   e. Declaration of policy
   f. Selection of objectives

2 *Foreign company risk factors*
   a. Company structure
   b. Capitalization
      1. Physical assets
      2. Operational resources
      3. Secondary resources
      4. Liquidity
   c. Trading history
   d. Market position
      1. Competitive share
      2. Potential share
      3. Capabilities
      4. Exposure to market factors

3 *Ownership and management*
   a. Background data
   b. Profiles
   c. Reputations
   d. Offices and functions

4 *External circumstances*
   a. Foreign government structure
   b. Policy and stability
   c. Competitive pressures
   d. Economy
      1. Industrial, commercial, agricultural
      2. Diversification, expansion potential
      3. Balance of trade
      4. Raw materials, exports/imports

5. Technology
6. Unskilled, semi-skilled and skilled labour
7. Union/management relations

e. Foreign jurisdicial features
1. Tribunals, administrative bodies
2. Litigation, submission of claims
3. Jurisdiction, persons and property
4. Civil law, statutes, decrees and decisions
5. Criminal law, procedure, liability and penalties.
6. Executive, legislative and judicial controls over trade, commerce, industry finance, taxation and currency

Tactics are strategy's tools. Like all tools they have a number of specialized functions, to which the art of the user imparts his individual skill. The negotiator's art is essential to the effective exposition of negotiating tacts; and so far as they pertain to international negotiations the tactics demand a high appreciation of the personality of the foreign adversary, the circumstances of the transaction, and the limitations upon the negotiator's available time. This last requirement is exacting far beyond its domestic counterpart because the international negotiator does not have at his disposal the comparative leisure afforded within his home market. More importantly, his foreign adversary is perfectly well aware of this kind of pressure, and, most of all, has the advantage, a very considerable one, of doing business within a familiar home surrounding. It need be mentioned only in passing that tactical tools are not self-executing instruments. They depend on the resources of the negotiator for their efficacy.

From what has been observed in the foregoing pages it must be clear that the negotiator must always conduct his bargaining within the cultural dimensions of the place. His selection of tactical measures aimed at convincing the other side is largely dictated by the psychological traits of his foreign adversary. This means that from the outset he must satisfy himself of the personal strengths and weaknesses, the susceptibilities that will enable him to use his tools well.

Stated otherwise, the negotiator must hunt out evidence of behavioural predictability, minimize false steps and maximize, however slowly, the right approach to final contract.

The basic tactics are simple, logical and the foundation for whatever techniques lie withing the negotiator's command.

Tactic 1. Open communications
Tactic 2. Establish personal rapport
Tactic 3. Arouse responsiveness
Tactic 4. Explore motivations
Tactic 5. Offer incentives and rewards

Correctly developed, tactics 1 to 5 evolve naturally and lead to agreement upon agreement, 'connection' after 'connection'. Not every foreign business permits, or even entails the need for, equal emphasis to be placed on each tactic. The negotiator's discretion, like the physician's, will guide him to what should be the right tactical application.

Strategy

The easiest way to look at strategy is by visualizing a number of targets. Each target is an objective. Each target is the subject of its own strategy. All the targets include all of the objectives, and the overall strategy sums up whatever the value of those target-objectives is. Some targets are of first importance. Others are secondary, and so on. Some targets must be taken. Others may be forgone. Strategy controls tactics. No strategy can succeed without tactical implementation. Tactics without strategy are pointless.

Intelligence, in the military sense, is critical to selection of targets, the application of strategy, and the employment of tactics. Tactics must conform to the local situation. What is appropriate to a negotiation for the acquisition of a franchise to operate a chain of vending machines in Belgium may not be at all relevant to a negotiation looking for points of sale outlets; introducing self-service food shops in Holland requires a different negotiating tactical order from setting up a hotel gambling concession in Santo Domingo. But whatever the transaction may cover, even two apparently similar ones, the tactics should be tailored to the controlling local conditions. If the local conditions differ at the two negotiating sites, then the tactics must vary with them.

Both for strategy and tactics, hard information is indispensable. The purpose of commanding all available sources of intelligence is to economize the negotiating procedures in point of time and impact. Where the information flow-chart shows probable agreement as to the strategic objectives, then the tactics may be soft-pedalled. Where on the other hand, the foreign adversary will oppose the objectives in dead earnest, then the negotiator should use the flow chart to work around the difficulties.

It is not necessary to adhere to any particular form of intelligence organization. So long as vital information can be gathered, appraised, and used effectively, the negotiator has ample room to set up any kind of information input that suits his negotiating style and techniques.

The following list is an example of an input scheme that will be a checklist for the negotiator's strategy and tactics. Wherever his incoming information fits the list, he can adapt himself to the local situation; if the information is inadequate, he will have to take special care to supply its deficiencies. The information categories are broad, substantive and elastic; they can be modified by extension or otherwise.

Tactic 1. Communications should always open on a non-controversial line in order to allay the hostility inherent in the foreign adversary. Change topics as often as necessary to establish an effective basis for personal exchanges that will reveal different perspectives without inflaming criticism.

Tactic 2. Develop the exchanges toward at least one area of accord. No matter how irrelevant the area, the negotiator should anchor his efforts at rapport within it, returning to it as often as necessary to ensure its reliability.

Tactic 3. Enlarge the adversary's confidence by feeding him questions that are simple, homely, personal. Get him to talk of himself, his family, his experience in general terms. Try to discover his preferences and prejudices. Lead him to initiate topics upon which agreement may be made smoothly.

Tactic 4. Focus on images that will crystallize his motivations. Try to induce him to define them and associate them within his official capacity; as he does this, swing the images over to the transaction. See what he expects to accomplish for himself by reaching contract.

Tactic 5. Develop his motivations as they relate to his company, and then analyze the positive side of the transaction so that, both from your viewpoint and his the terms and conditions of the negotiation can be equated to incentives and rewards accruing to him in consequence of the anticipated contract.

In addition to the foregoing, and in order to prepare the adversary for the possibility that you will have to insist on provisions that he might not have contemplated, or on such as may force him to modify his own expectations, or on those that will be questioned by his own company, lay out an optimum-agreement hypothesis which will test his willingness and authority to compromise. Draw him to participate in a colloquy such as 'Well, if we agree to do A, can we expect your company to do B? 'How close can we come to satisfying both sides? What can you recommend to your company, if I am ready to make parallel suggestions?' Let him understand your interest in building a relationship between both sides that will reach beyond the particular business in hand. Set the tone for the further bargaining so that disappointment will not be accompanied by distrust or rancour. The cushioning effect of the suggestion noted in the preceding paragraph is important. It lends a touch of 'realistic' qualification that may very well correspond to his own feeling of hope against hope that the transaction, even if short of his mark, may nevertheless pave the way to a future profitable relationship. In addition, it opens the door to a probable course of persuasion in which you must convince him that the revision of his position is practicable and the best that can be done in the circumstances. It will also permit you to (a) persuade him to agree to the substitution of modifications and (b) persuade him to forgo a penalty or bonus imposition on your company. This pre-conditioning cushion should be prepared without waving flags. If it is too bluntly phrased, the foreign adversary may feel that he is being taken in by an imminent 'bait and switch' device.

He should be comfortable in the feeling that your cushion is actually a friendly gesture. If he scents a let-down he may be hesitant to go farther for fear of criticism made by his company on the ground that he is not a 'strong' negotiator. Point out to him that it is better to make the transaction on best available terms than to report a 'no hits, no runs, no errors' score to his company. Let him see that you yourself are virtually in the same negotiating seat. This requires you to identify yourself with him and to bring him to believe that in your official role you play the same part he does.

The force of your personality ought to suffice for the purpose. In fact, it is possible to leave him with the impression more than enough latitude for accommodation. In fact, you may even succeed in having him consider it along the lines of a renegotiation insofar as you and he already have set up broad areas of general agreement. By bringing up your persuasive powers you can only draw him to your side, and if the proposed business has any reasonable prospect of advantage and profit he will be quick to join your arguments, or at the very least he will be aware of the importance of cooperating with you so that both companies can reach contract. In short, you will have eliminated any likelihood that at a later time he will charge you with having raised false hopes and let him down when the bargaining came to brass tacks. It cannot be stated too often that the outcome of a foreign negotiation is, to a far greater extent than at home, influenced by the negotiator's success in establishing a 'friendship bridge' with his foreign adversary. The exception, earlier mentioned, occurs in Eastern Bloc negotiations.

Technique, flair and style

Technique is what we practise, flair is what we have, and style is how we show it. 'In the grand manner' means the negotiator has associated to himself the presence of an outstanding personality; he has adopted it as his style. When we say 'He has the gift of the gab', we are remarking on someone's flair; we discern and designate an innate attribute. Again, as we note the skill used to insinuate and press home a suggestion we compliment the persuader's combination of psychological expertise and recognize it as the product of study, training and experience.

Technique can be acquired, adapted, revised, amplified, reformed. Whatever empirical information we find useful to international negotiation can be analyzed, synthesized and repeatedly engaged for our occasions abroad. We have one technique for sales, another for purchases. One technique comes handy in dealing with manufacturers, another with merchandisers. When in Portugal, we apply our persuasion through a technique particular to the time, place and circumstance. In Mexico, our technique takes another form. Sometimes during a single international transaction we may call upon several techniques, each of which will have been rehearsed countless times in similar situations.

Flair ordinarily means our ability to capitalize attractively certain inborn qualities that distinguish us from the thousands of other negotiators who, taken one by one, to some degree possess their own flair and other likewise recognizable terms as individuals to a greater or lesser degree shaped by an unusual eyebrow, a list, a loping gait, an attitude, a smile, a frown, a naive aspect, a certain *elan*, an indefinable self-confidence.

Style means manner. How we set ourselves before the foreign eye will characterize our style. If we prefer sweeping generalizations, broad strokes of assurance, vivid figures of speech, then our foreign adversary may see us 'in the grand manner. If we harp on trivia, he will say 'he is niggling' and believe us to be ridden by apprehension.

Combine a sound and appropriate technique with an acceptable idiosyncracy; express them with faultless suitability and the art of the international negotiator blossoms forth. The three elements, technique, flair and style are modular in the sense that technique may be changed while flair is retained and style modified. Flair may be suppressed while technique and style are modified. Techniques may be substituted for each other to suit the circumstances abroad and the particular personality of the foreign adversary. The upshot of our art is persuasion. So we must be able to diagnose the susceptibilities of our opponent and play to them. They vary with the place, with the language, with the culture. We must be able to fashion our techniques, flair and style to fit the occasion.

If our technique must use a soft-sell approach in Normandy, a hard-sell one in Sicily, an involved and scientific one in Bavaria, an easy suggestive one in Northumberland, our job is to meet the necessity of the occasion. If the way we stuff our pipe with tobacco displays us as thoughtful, and hence attractive in New England, then by all means let us engage in pipe-filling, puffing and whatever else adds to our theatrical preparation. Should tone, inflection, apparent spontaneity be valued in Paris, then that's the flair to be linked to us. If a phrase is important as a mark of our social rank, sophistication and distinction, let there be no feeling of hesitation: say the right phrase. It's all part of the art. The international negotiator must acept himself as a dramatic figure, as an advocate, as a musical and graphic artist, capable of rendering his conceptual images in comprehensible language so that the adversary will almost literally see and be convinced by them.

When we are abroad, for as long as we stay, until our negotiations end, we are visible and audible, utterly exposed to the locals. We are practically touched, prodded and pushed by them in their need and wish to know who we are and how we differ from them. So we must show ourselves to best advantage. They test us by little things. Do we keep appointments punctually in Frankfurt? That's a good sign there. Are we impatient when our adversary is late in Vienna? Do we show it? If so, that's a bad sign. Examples multiply with every experience. The fundamental thing to remember about technique is that 'once is not enough'. It should be inspected, oiled, rehearsed, tested time after time. The thing to remember about flair is that at different places the lisp, the obtrusive 'r', the stammer may be seen as signs of decent modesty — at others as signals of effiminacy. Suppress the flair if necessary. Style can be altered or adopted without any difficulty. Find the right one for the right time and adversary, then wear it as if it were your own. When you move on, test the negotiating atmosphere and suit your style to what will go down well with the locals.

Everything that has anything to do with the art of international negotiation comes down to the point of deciding what kind of mental and emotional attitude will influence the adversary to agree on terms and conditions.

No matter how the question is stated, the answer always lies in establishing a control over him. This is what we seek to do by eye-dominance, gaining the psychological ascendancy by out-staring our adversary in an 'eyeball to eyeball' contest. We feel triumphant when we get him to lower his lids, turn away, or imperceptibly and somewhat unconsciously nod his head. We are delighted when we test our ocular perception, seize the initiative to break off the contest, resume it, recontrol him and then lead into a vocal dominance. Then we raise or lower our tone of address, increase or decrease the rate of speech, mumble or whisper, shout or return to normal levels of conversation — always, drawing our adversary to follow suit, again demonstrating dominance. It is like playing a trout in a stream. Does it always succeed? No. But the percentage of partial success can be impressive. And this dominance-objective can make an ordinary

Mr Milquetoast look like Richard the Lion Heart for as long as is necessary to close the deal, fold the tent and steal away without looking back. Those whose modesty prevents them from experimenting with controlled situations might get their feet wet in these psychological waters by remembering that their job is to go to contract by any fair means. And no damage is done if they put on a brave show, march off with the contract at dawn. No danger lies in calculated haste; on the contrary it prevents the adversary from pulling his beard and thinking it all over. Dominance techniques vary. They should not be used indiscriminately. Their optimal function is as a kind of psychological litmus paper, telling the negotiator just how hard or soft his foreign adversary may be, how far he can be led, how far he must be pushed, and how far the negotiator must take him on the road of proof. In other words, dominating the adversary is something close to giving your boxing opponent the 'evil eye' in order to instill the fear of the Lord in him. But you must yet deliver the clincher, and that takes another technique.

Follow up the superior/inferior opening with a close observation of his behaviour. If he doodles, try to see what they are. If he fidgets, see what caused him to do so. Then, if it is something you said, do it again. Maybe it is your tone of voice. Repeat it. If he crosses and uncrosses his legs, he is trying to resist you. Should you wish to reduce his resistance, alter your style. If you wish to increase his resistance, stress whatever you have been doing to vex him. If you are trying to upset him, confuse him and arouse him to a commitment of one or another kind by some counter-aggressive act, alternate your attack. Change topics. Break off before you complete one of them. Drop your voice. Make him lean forward. Do it again. Get up. Walk away. Take a cigar; look out of the window. Remember a pressing appointment. In short, hit him from every angle — but do it politely. Try explaining some phase of the business. Interrupt it by asking him whether he understands you. If he does, go on to another topic, but not before you ask him 'Are you sure?' This, said helpfully, can irritate him and make him seethe because of your implication that he is not capable of receiving and grasping your over-simple explanation of an uncomplicated matter concerned with his own business.

All this can be done within your own convenient time-span. In fact, it is almost essential to do it earliest, say within the first half-hour, if possible. This permits you to act as the rough detective, at the outset; then, for the rest of the negotiation you can take the part of the sweet-reasoned soft detective. Your adversary, depending on your adriot handling, will be eating out of your hand, cultivating your kind opinion of him, and ready to sign anything you place before his myopic, disconcerted countenance.

Further on what we may call physical techniques, the great thing to keep in mind is that you are not to take your pleasure too far. Your task is to build 'connections' not combats. So, the minute you have worked your way through your psychological muscle exhibit, seat yourself in front of the foreign adversary and smile. You have nothing to lose. He will respond with a smile. Good. No contest. On the other hand, if he does not, and only glowers at you, you are still ahead because (a) he does not understand what you are driving at, or (b) he fears you. Tell him to draw his chair closer to you. If he does, the rest is as easy as pie. For he is literally doing what the courting chimpanzees do when they mate. You will have only to return to non-controversial topics, and then the road is clear all the way to your smiling suggestion: 'Well, since we understand each other, let's take a look at the ball of wax and see what the bees are saying'. Out come your memoranda, and since he will be cornered into 'yes', 'no' alternatives, you can reframe your proposals comfortably, having settled the main question, that the transaction is beyond controversy, except for ironing out details'.

The 'good detective' sequence is a form of reward that takes us farther in our presentation. Admittedly, there are times when the road to contract is not paved with easy acceptance. Assuming the existence of negotiating obstacles that are purely personal, the obvious course to follow is that of reaching a community of interest on a personal basis. Try to get the foreign adversary's reaction to some peripheral index, such as an appreciation of open golf tournaments, as opposed to purely amateur matches. Go from there to the tremendous popularity of tennis in recent years. Whatever you raise for conversation purposes can be used to throw light on his value-judgment standards. It is immensely urgent for you to know what he uses as a base-line for 'normality'. While it may not be absolutely correct to expect him to define himself in terms of 'normality', indeed, he may be perplexed by the question, you can go from insight to another on this topic by using golf or tennis or football as a stepping-stone, keeping in mind that at some turn of the exchange you want to find out what he considers 'normal'. The reason for this is that once you can establish his reference to normality, then you can project his general response to a standard; and, finally, you can zero in on your expectations of what he would regard as normal in relation to your proposals. In other words, by deriving a clue, you can almost foresee what his attitude will be when you come down to the proposals. His attitude will guide you to an understanding of how the terms and conditions should be agreed.

To be certain, 'normality' is social, regional, economic, permanent, temporary, figurative; it is rarely an absolute. And since it is a comparative, it is important when dealing with a foreign adversary to be able to draw a connection between his sight of normality and your own. Otherwise you will find the disconcerting conclusion that many foreign business conferences come to: that is to say, your adversary, with all good will, rises to stretch himself just before putting pen to paper and asks you to specify which set of normalities you were speaking of, those relating to his country, your country, or the country where the contract will be performed? This question is straightforward — but trying to meet it at the end of the conversations is like trying to take flypaper off one hand by using another. The negotiation can fall apart simply because, too late, opposing critical standards cannot be settled, at any rate they cannot be easily disposed of without having to pass over the entire subject matter; and this can fuel a feeling of dissatisfaction.

It is helpful to fix the adversary's view of normality within the context of his culture. This supplies us an insight into what the foreign company may be expected to do in agreeing contract, and, later, in performing it. Predictability is critically important.

Cultural context must be weighed so that 'normal' is not mistakenly applied. If, as happened to be the case in a certain transaction with a Belgian steel executive, the adversary had a penchant for dyeing his hair electric-blue and taking his economic views from a palm-reader, the behavioural pattern is miles apart from that of the negotiator, 'normal' and 'predictable' must be corrected to the cultural context abroad. A step further into this area takes us to a consideration of the reality of a foreign negotiation where both sides know the ropes pretty well and preliminary sparring on innocuous topics shows little or nothing of the inner thoughts of either party. The negotiator in such cases should abandon the non-controversial topics and strive to stir up a lively chat on others that will be more fruitful. Whether the new line is scientific or speculative does not matter as much as its potential for putting the adversary's personal standards in a cultural perspective. There need be no sacrifice of amicability or courtesy in pursuing this enquiry. If the enquiry is followed, he should learn many things otherwise unknown to him that concern his adversary's standards, aesthetic preferences, prosaic tastes, political orientation, religious affiliations, financial standing, social connections, company ambitions and professional expertise. These are relevant areas of enquiry — and all of them lead to an evaulation of the adversary's standards. Some of them may have been covered in the company's information dealing with the foreign company and its leading personalities. But any new information can be useful as a clue to what the foreign adversary, Swedish, Australian, Swiss, Japanese, French or otherwise, may believe to be correct, just, binding and enforcible. Likely enough each of the nationals noted above will hold standards that are similar to those held by the others in some particulars and dissimilar in such as touch culturally distinct experience. The stereotypical image is a good point of departure. The controversial wedge will be a mine of additional material. Combining the two surely should supply the negotiator with more than enough reliable information upon which to calculate whether the ngeotiations hold prospects for eventual agreement, and also whether the negotiations can be contained within a given period of time.

What inferences can be drawn about the predictability of the following subject?

> Alysius Schindler, born Alsace-Lorraine, 1938; graduate Sorbonne 1960, M.I.T. (US) 1964 (aeronaut. engr); economic analyst, Haiti, for French bank; employed: Boeing (US), Heinckel (Germ), aerodynamics. Managing Dr, La Plata Aircraft Products, Rio de Janeiro, 2 yrs; now ass't to chairman of bd, Banco Real, Caracas. Engaged to chairman's daughter. Likes Mozart, dislikes Lalo.

As a stereotypical Alsatian, the subject is a hard, deliberate decision-maker; at the Sorbonne he would be exposed to Liberal socialist views; at M.I.T., he was in contact with the latest US aerodynamic technology; his employment record is conservative and consistent; he probably has tri-lingual fluency; his managerial experience and scientific background is useful in opening personal opportunity for advancement socially and otherwise. His function as an economic analyst provided insight into capital structure of company operations; travel and cosmopolitan experience are useful socially and the marriage will consolidate personal and social position, perhaps providing a springboard to the chairmanship of his father-in-law's bank.

A number of other conclusions can be drawn by the reader; those suggested suffice to draw a conclusion of predictable conservatism, adherence to cosmopolitan standards, and a sense of normality within a European/South American orbit, modified by study period and work in the United States. No indication of irregularity warranted. Preference for Mozart as opposed to Lalo supports expectation of strict conformity to regular course of negotiation. No present basis for supposing that Schindler would risk criticism, unpleasant publicity or embarrassment by ill-considered ventures. If agreed, contract would be appropriately supervised to ensure legality at inception and during performance.

The subject could just as well be a Mr Schindler from Dayton, Ohio, if he became an American citizen. Highly respectable member of establishment, he would need little or no adjustment to his concepts of commerce or to his negotiating patterns. And as Mr Schindler of Manchester, he would only have to join the local tennis club to be readily accepted. Wherever he would be, at home or abroad, his motives, objectives, ambitions and activities would be representative of an educated, cultivated, scientific mind that would be focussed on practicability, with little or no risk. Predictability evaluation better than average for straightforward contract negotiation.

Any consideration of the formation, selection and use of negotiating techniques in international markets must lead to the conclusion that the demands on the negotiator are more rigorous than they are at home. The interaction of external and internal economic pressures is so fluid that the transactional situation can change in hours, sometimes even in minutes — and the internationalist must be immediately responsive to any change in order to carry out the mission in hand, and to protect it from a limitless variety of unforeseeable and uncontrollable misadventures.

Vast fields of information must be at his disposal. Communications must be maintained with his domestic company. Relations with his foreign adversary must be regulated on a course that can be seen as objective. Criticism for imprudent or rash acts can prejudice the negotiations; and the acts can precipitate more serious consequences. In this atmosphere of doing business, the negotiator must exercise faultless, or nearly faultless judgment, in deciding what kind of technique can be best selected and applied for the completion of his work.

The selection of technique places the negotiator at risk if the approach does not succeed. But the technique by itself is not enough. The right technique must be accompanied by the right talent and manner. In some places abroad, excessive flattery is the key to turn the doorkeeper's consent. In others it is important to maintain humourless gravity; and in still others the opening of any transaction hinges on a nice command of formal rhetorical expositions of the origins of the proposed enterprise, the reasons why it had come to be accepted as a workable plan, and, finally, the advantages and profits that will accrue to the benefit of all the concerned parties.

It is unnecessary to attempt to catalogue techniques, country by country; it would be futile to try to do so. For each international negotiator must evolve his own approaches. No two individuals bear more than a cursory resemblance to each other. No two transactions are alike. Nor are the negotiating conditions abroad constant. Whether for political, economic or social change, taken singly or all together, the foreign market demands inventive, imaginative, effectual improvization; some techniques, by definition, must be crystallized in repetitive patterns. Others, obviously must be created on the spot. Negotiation in the new Third World countries is different from the conventional transaction of business elsewhere. Techniques to suit the differences must be seen as more than pouring old wine into new bottles.

Chapter 9

Administration and procedure

Credentials; authority; power; discretion; statements; representations; facts; figures and statistics; predictability; establishing principles and limitations; options and alternatives

For the sake of confidentiality, security and essential secrecy the negotiator must assure himself of the foreign adversary's right to act for the foreign company. He should also be able to offer proof supporting his official position abroad on behalf of the domestic company. The way to do this is by presenting, and demanding, effective evidence of accreditation. A careful inspection of the exchanged documentation is in order and should not be waived because of embarrassed hesitation. Getting the transaction off on the right foot cannot be resented, and should not be underestimated. Often enough a negotiation rolls along on the assumption, misplaced, that the negotiator is face to face with a representative of the intended foreign company when, in fact, the case is otherwise.

Three reasons for caution should suffice:

1. Accreditation identifies the participants and prevents fraud; it also enables the negotiator to determine whether the adversary can actually negotiate, or is limited to receiving offers.
2. Accreditation screens the participants and excludes from the conference persons having no acceptable interest in learning the nature of the transaction.
3. Accreditation preserves privacy with particular respect to trade matters, projects, policy and confidential material, while protecting the domestic company against espionage or premature leakage of its undertakings.

Ordinarily, the nature of the accreditation can be provided

by prior agreement in communications arranging the negotiation. If there is doubt about the sufficiency of the proof of identity and power to deal, the negotiator can ask for a range of items, such as the following:

1. Company and personal visiting cards
2. Copies of preceding correspondence
3. Identity cards and official national registrations
4. Copies of automobile insurance policies
5. Circular letters, letters of reference (bank)
6. Embassy or consular letters of introduction
7. Passports, photograph, entry and exit permits
8. Code-forms keyed to company blacklight screening
9. Police clearance approval, with fingerprints
10. Local verification by official bureaux

In view of the high incidence of commercial conspiracies, improper surveillance by government officials and rival companies, it is to the negotiator's interest to guard his company against 'unauthorized intervention'; his caution will be respected. On foreign soil anything can happen, and it is essential to avoid disclosure of information and, as well, the unwelcome presence of persons having no proper business at the negotiation.

Authority, power and discretion

Negotiating authority cannot be taken for granted. It must be established explicitly; and the negotiator should enquire whether or not the foreign company has in truth authorized the foreign adversary (a) to exchange proposals, and (b) to settle them into an agreement. Relying on accreditation is not enough. It may be adequate as identification but deficient in extent. Thoroughness in ascertaining authority will save well-intended negotiators from mistaking the person before them as the person who has the authority to act.

Power must coincide with authority. So the negotiator must pursue the preliminary examination by asking his adversary whether his authority to negotiate is coupled to a power of decision, a power of contract-execution, or a power — as often happens — only to refer the transaction to a higher officer within the foreign company. The appearance of power can be deceptive. Sometimes the foreign adversary's ego presses him to attempt to act in excess of his power in order to bring off a deal, as in those instances where he attends on behalf of the foreign company but his presence is limited to 'observation'.

Assuming that accreditation, authority and power have been established, the negotiator must yet learn whether the adversary has any discretion to vary the negotiating frame of reference. In Eastern Bloc countries, discretion to do so simply does not exist. In others it is ambulatory, varying from place to place and foreign company to foreign company. Accepting a verbal assurance may suffice if a memorandum is made of the assurance. The adversary's 'If I say I can do it, it means I can do it' is not always the gospel truth; and the negotiator ought to exercise his common sense toward certainty when the transaction involves or seems to involve the adversary's use of discretion.

Statements and representations

Since foreign business takes its cue from an exchange of communications between two different cultures, two different behavioural patterns, as expressed across two different languages, bargaining must be checked and rechecked to distinguish between outright declarations, statements, representations and puffing. Obviously, each side is pointing toward a contract, and each side will say things to support its aim. The purpose is inducement, and if it is innocent it may withal be misleading. Often it is not innocent and does mislead. It is the negotiator's responsibility to separate the contractual wheat from the verbal chaff. It can do no harm if he bears in mind the elements of deceit, and uses them to test the declarations made to him by the other side. They may alert him to the possibility that he is being deceived. These elements are:

1. A statement that is false when made.
2. It was false to the knowledge of the speaker.
3. It was made to induce the negotiator to rely on it.
4. The negotiator having no knowledge of the truth or falsity of the statement, relied and acted on it.
5. The negotiator changed his position in reliance on the statement, and was caused (or his principal was caused) to sustain injury and damage.

the negotiator should be careful that his own declarations of representations, but generally they are linked together, and are so treated in resulting law suits. There are certain declarations, either as representations and statements that are borderline, just skirting but not entering the field of fraud and deceit. These are referred to as 'opinions' or 'matters of opinion'. Especially because of the cultural and linguistic gulf between the transactors, it is most important for the negotiator to be exact in his understanding of what the other side's declarations amount to. At home it is easy to distinguish between 'I believe', 'I think', 'I have a feeling', 'It is my opinion', 'I have been told', on the one hand, and all declarations that are affirmative as expositions of fact. Even so, the lawbooks are replete with judicial decisions that split hairs between opinion and fact declarations. Abroad, it is imperative to be precise in grasping whether a declaration is precatory, as 'I trust it will go well', or declaratory, 'I know it will go well', 'I give you my word it will go well', 'It will go well', and similar assurances made factually. There is an infinite number of troublesome cases rising from opinions that have been construed as strong declarations. And the negotiator should be careful that his own declarations of opinion do not fall into the grey areas. For if they do, his company may smart for his carelessness. One point more: declarations should be checked bi-lingually. The negotiator cannot permit himself to be told that he has committed his company through carelessness on his part, or on that of his interpreter. There is no warrant for a cavalier attitude toward 'fine print' words and phrases, particularly oral ones. As a practical matter, what the negotiator should do is ask himself how, at home, he would treat the adversary's declaration. And he can reverse the test, and ask himself how his own declarations might be treated in the foreign country's language.

Speaking of grey areas, one of the difficult ones lies in incomplete statements that seem to say a good deal, but, actually take their appearance of completeness from a flourish of arms, or a wink, or a nod, or a posture. If it is not spoken, if it is not written, the negotiator ought not to assume it to be a declaration or a statement or a representation. The other side can readily say 'You understood more than I meant', or 'You misunderstood me', or 'You understood what you chose to understand, not what I said'.

Where the other side makes declarations that are patently false, the negotiator has several options. He can refute them. He can call for accurate statements. He can close his briefcase and walk away. He can sit tight and disregard the deception, or treat it as innocent or immaterial. Sometimes declarations are overblown in order to discover how much the other side knows. Where the declarations are openly unfounded in truth, or where they are half-truths, or consist in concealments, the negotiator — assuming he detects them — should elect to challenge them. The outcome might be surprising.

In Germany while negotiating at a plant in Cologne, the author was given a number of written representations that were examined and found inaccurate. He decided to continue the negotiating on the following day, after having verified the true state of affairs. He then demanded a fresh set of representations. They were handed over immediately. They had been prepared in advance by the German company, apparently on the expectation that if the initial representations were rejected, it would save time to have the right ones at hand. There was no embarrassment or apology by the foreign negotiator. The ploy had been planned, presented and failed. *Les affaires sont les affaires* was the attitude. The negotiation concluded on correct terms, and everyone parted amicably. The author was even paid a flattering compliment on his ability to detect the impropriety of the representations first offered to him. He accepted it with tongue in cheek and left.

Facts, figures and statistics

Facts, figures and statistics relevant to an international negotiation may be agreed. When they do not meet a challenge, no problem arises. When they do, the negotiator's task is to place them in the light he wishes them to be seen. In a sense it takes him back to the philosophical perspective. A cup may be 'half empty' or 'half full', according to the issue. So, a fact must be seen from the same standpoint in order to gain accord. In other words, it is useless to argue for or against the adversary's fact without understanding his premise. This does not compel agreement, but it does bridge the controversy with a way toward agreement. For the negotiator's presentation of facts that may or will be questioned, it is advisable to have authoritative support not only on the facts in issue but on the correct or preferred way to treat them. Conversely, the adversary's claim of fact must be met by authoritative opposition, especially when he will come armed with authorities.

As to figures, the old saw that 'figures don't lie, but liars figure' says all that is needed to induce the negotiator to examine not only the adversary's figures and sources of information but his credibility; to overlook credibility is to invite being overreached. Statistics in the ordinary way are arrangements of facts through numerical, graphic or symbolic substitutes. That they include conclusions should be remarked as worthy of notice. Conclusions are fallible, even when the raw information appears unimpeachable. First of all, the statistics may be correct, but not fully representative. Secondly, the events or conditions meant to be reflected may be transient or non-operative. Thirdly, the statistician's motive for selectivity should be examined. Clearly the purpose of statistical reportage is to demonstrate the existence or non-existence, the possibility or impossibility, the probability or improbability of something. The statistic, in short, is formed to frame a purpose. Knowing the purpose is a guide to the validity of the statistic. So-called impartial statistics may be attacked where the calculations are suspected of being slanted; and this applies equally to those tendered by the negotiator and such as are produced by his adversary. The ultimate application of care rests in the facts, figures and statistics, of any sort, that will find their way into the contract. Currency, terms of payment, qualitative and quantitative requirements must be identified against a uniform or agreed standard, and that standard is to be expressed in the contract. Tons should not be mistaken for tonnes, pounds for kilograms; positive reference to currency as of the time and place of payment is essential, and so on.

Not only must the kind of fact be defined, but it must be rendered certain or capable of ascertainment free of doubt. This requirement goes to the intentions of the contracting parties most particularly in international negotiations. The negotiator must at all times remember that every foreign-made agreement holds a greater or lesser degree of potential litigation within its four corners. And legality rest on clarity. If a contractual fact, figure or statistic cannot be deduced from the writings and engagements, then it will be treated as cause for determining that the parties failed to reach a meeting of the minds on the material elements of their proposed contract. It is to the negotiator's interest to reach a valid and enforcible agreement, not to embroider it with imprecision. In such transactions that relate to descriptive material of a technical nature, the negotiator should advantage himself by having the contract refer to that material, and thereby incorporating it by reference. Where variations are prefigured, then the range of variation should be agreed as a fact and specified within plus-minus limitations. Certainty, definition, ascertainability, and authoritative references are all helpful in giving factual reality to the foreign contract. The omission of important figures or statistical support can only hamper the parties' performance of their obligations and thereby give rise to ill will.

Establishing principles and limitations

In further aid of specificity, the negotiator ought to think of the ground rules that will shape the transaction. If, for example, the agreement depends on the existence of a certain tariff — but subject to tariff revision, then the negotiator should see to it that the extent of revision is defined within a tolerance. The revision, as and when it occurs can then be measured against what the parties prefigured; if it does not impair their calculations, the contract performance can continue; if it does, assuming adequate provision for such an event is drafted into the contract, then the contract can be terminated, rescinded, annulled, voided, or deemed discharged — whichever is the method indicated in the contract itself. Again, where there is a likelihood that partial performance may feature the course of the contract, the parties should deal with it, specifying the terms and conditions that will comprise 'partial', or 'substantial' compliance, and providing liquidated payments in lieu of full performance. Similarly, where the engagement turns on the existence of an inventory of raw materials, the parties might avoid later dispute by arranging for the quantities and qualifications of the materials as of the time that the contract is to take effect. And where the rendering of accounts between the parties is to be fixed, the time should be made certain as to day, month and year; to the same effect is the time required for the giving or receipt of notice, the performance of an act, the time of extension for a renewal, the exercise of an option of any kind, and the occurrence of any contingent even contemplated by the parties as the trigger for the discharge of their duties to each other.

Limitations should be foreseen not only with regard to the course of the negotiations, the performance of the agreed contract, the relations of the parties during the term of contract, but also with a prospective eye toward their relations on its conclusion. For it must accepted that every contract creates radiating consequences that affect the parties long after they have respectively carried out their undertakings. So, as an example, where the negotiator engages the foreign company to manufacture an article under license, he should agree with the other side as to the right of the foreign company to manufacture the article for its own account after the date of termination. Or, of course, he may take the opposite view, restraining the other side from that kind of activity. This restraint, and others that aim at a similar protection, may be considered as covenants that are negative. Negative covenants affect various aspects of industrial, commercial and financial relationships. It may be necessary to protect a territory, conserve a trade list, provide exclusivity for the use of a method. Patents and trademarks fall within the theory of negative protection, although the exclusivity they grant is a creature of law, either common or statutory.

The true basis of protecting exclusivity is knowledge. In international matters, like those at home, what is sought to be shielded by the restraint is some kind of knowledge. A director's access to inside information, an employee's familiarity with a working model, a shareholder's acquaintance with a company proposal, indeed almost every economic relationship, may merit restraint. The restraints vary with the case. Salesman ceasing employment may be restrained from making use of a customer list, or a number of resources for additional parts, or of a potential improvment in a distributive system. The restraint always has to be reasonable, usually is for a period of time appropriate to the economic activity, and ordinarily covers a specifically designated geographical area, such as a village, town, country, province, country — or group of countries, as in a common market community. The main thing to remember is that all restraints must be suited to the nature of the relationship and should not contravene reasonableness or offend morality. So, where the relationship was confined to a city, it is reasonable to limit the restraint to the city; it is unreasonable to work a restraint barring the restrained party from pursuing his employment or business elsewhere in the country. Examples can be multiplied, but the reader can suppose them easily enough.

However, negotiations present a special case because the information sought and tendered during the bargaining period may, if the transaction falls through, be used improperly by one party against another. And in foreign business this can work serious and irreparable injury. Many unscrupulous persons open negotiations as if they were sincere, but use them as fishing expeditions to pry into the affairs of the opposite party. If the negotiator is careless, his company will be seriously disadvantaged, and, what is more, without remedy. What should be done by his company beforehand, and often is, can be simple and effective: the domestic company should make the transaction abroad hinge on an explicit agreement by the foreign company to hold private any and all information it derives from the negotiation. This places the foreign company under a double duty. First, it will be held to its agreement as a contractual undertaking. Second, if it violates the agreement and deceit can be established, the domestic company can have recourse for deceit and fraud in a tort action. The breach of privacy, confidentiality, or secrecy can be punished by a judgment for damages, and, in some cases other penalties may be imposed on the offending foreign company.

Options and alternatives

The protection of information can be safeguarded by another device. At the outset of the negotiation abroad, the foreign company should be drawn to agreement that if the transaction fails to mature, it may use the information gained in the exchange provided it pays to the domestic company a certain sum of money as consideration (or as liquidated damages) for such an option. If it decides not to exercise the option, then it will be bound to the highest degree of secrecy, forbidden to make any disclosure of any kind to any person without the prior written consent of the domestic company. This kind of provision takes on the character of *in terrorem* clauses, but it is important to look ahead and supply at the outset the protection that may be later needed but unavailable. The device is also a good test of the genuine motives of the foreign company in taking part in the negotiation. Thus, where the domestic company negotiates in France for a real property development to go forward at Cap d'Antibes, and the French company decides not to enter into the scheme, the knowledge it gained of the project is valuable information and the domestic company might later discover that the French company has decided to work the scheme for its own advantage, has staked out the land it learned was valuable, and is assembling the parcels of land that originally were selected by the domestic company for the purpose.

One way to deal with such a situation in advance is to set up an alternative that will keep the foreign company 'honest'. Prepare two schemes, one, let us say at Cap d'Antibes, and the other for Le Toquet. Have the preliminary architect's renderings, photographs of the sites, land surveys, and municipal approval all in good order; then present both schemes to the foreign company. Use a memorandum or letter of intent to be signed by the foreign company in which it agrees that it has seen all of the said material, that it has viewed it with the object of choosing either or agreeing both schemes. After this is done, should the foreign company fail to follow through in the negotiations, the domestic company's proof of priority will enable it to get a restraint against the foreign company as to both schemes if it chooses. Should the foreign company violate the information it acquired and seek to capitalize on it, the domestic company can pursue its remedy on one scheme while going into developmenton the other. In such instances, the need to set up a feint or 'straw' scheme is obvious for ideas, as such cannot be protected; but it is something else in cases where the information is hard, as evidenced by (a) the prepared materials, and (b) the steps taken by the domestic company in furtherance of its project. The domestic company could properly urge that the sole purpose of the foreign company's negotiating presence was to improperly procure private information as applicable to a particular system of land development.

No guarantee of the efficacy of alternatives can be made. The axiom that for every wrong there is a remedy is too pat; the converse, really, is true: for every remedy there is a newly devised wrong. But the negotiator should be alerted to the need to create some alternative to defend his company against 'intellectual' piracy. Doubtless, once he sees the problem he can provide a useful solution. The main thing is to see the problem of unauthorized brain-picking.

Chapter 10

Closing the contract

Main instruments and collateral papers; referential materials; drafting provisos; execution and record keeping; bi-lingual conformity; copies and distribution

Main instruments

At the end of the international negotiation, the agreed terms and conditions should be reduced to writing. Preferably the final contracting papers will be bi-lingual renderings. As at home, the recitals will identify the parties by name and structure (partnership, company and so on), setting out the principal places of business for each side. The rights and duties will be particularized as agreed. Where appropriate, remedies and the forum for their application may be indicated. Supplemental writings should be annexed to the main contract to give substance to collateral undertakings, such as chattel mortgages, bills of exchange, and so on. References to letters of credit, warehouse receipts, and all forms of commercial instruments made part of the bargain ought to be carefully phrased in terms consonant with the law of the place where the contractual obligations are to be carried out.

While the negotiator is not himself required to know the force and effect of foreign law, he must see to it that the contract complies with the legal requirements both at the place where, on behalf of his company, he will execute it, and at the place where it will be performed. This means that competent legal opinion on these heads will be taken. 'Taken' means that he will receive it from some source other than the foreign company's lawyers. Obviously, it would be ill-considered to look to them to protect his company; and doubtless ethical considerations would restrain them from doing so. Nevertheless, he should not rely on their views, given ethically or not. His company should make available whatever legal advice is requisite for the transaction's definition within the formal papers.

Referential materials

All quantitative and qualitative norms and standards, all surveys, analytical reports, tests, measurements, certifications, codes, correspondence, international treaty provisos, patent and copyright attestations, assignments of interest, deeds, trial balance sheets, profit and loss statements, annual company statements, government licenses, permits, credit appraisals, architect's renderings, building plans, municipal ordinances, conference minutes, of any sort should be mentioned to the extent that they have been specified and particularized in the main contract. Where useful, copies of them should be annexed in toto.

Where required for safety, accessibility or foreign compliance, the main instruments should be registered at the appropriate office, such as that of a foreign notary. The right to refer to said papers, copy and withdrawal for purposes including litigation ought to be mentioned in the main contract.

It may be cumbersome and awkward to provide all of the materials; undoubtedly many foreign matters are completed sketchily, and often enough satisfactorily. But the negotiator must act defensively whenever he can. If the foreign adversary decries the special pains taken, the objection should be noted but not accepted, unless, of course, the risk is worth taking.

Generally, it is the foreign adversary who exercises fine-combed inspection of the contract's final wording. Frequently, the interpreters for both sides can cooperate toward preparing a satisfactory draft. More often than not, foreign counsel employs bi-lingual secretaries who are experienced in reducing commercial language to paper with faultless accuracy. But even so, the negotiator must be dead certain that the contracting papers are rock-ribbed, water-tight and free from troublesome ambiguities, omissions and plain error.

If the foreign negotiator generously offers to see to the drafting, the answer should be negative. First of all, it is not the negotiator's right to entrust this important operation to his opponent. Secondly, doing so creates a temptation for the foreign adversary that is unfair — he must not be placed on the spot. And it would, in such circumstances, be irresistible for him to select some word or phrase which, even by a hair, would favour the foreign company. The chance for mistake by him would be obvious, the temptation apparent, and the occasion for damage too enticing. The negotiator, in any event, ought not to show himself as careless, guileless, ingenuous or plainly foolish.

There is something else to be noted. The written contract should reflect all of the matters agreed, and it should record them in writing within the intent of both sides. There ought to be no division between what was orally settled and what appears in the main and collateral papers. Sometimes, when there is a disparity and it is called to the attention of the other side, the foreign negotiator may say 'Ah well, that's just a technicality', or 'I'm so sorry, but we'll have to leave it that way; my secretary's gone for the day'. Whatever the reason, the negotiator must not proceed until and unless the difference between what was said and what is written is reconciled appropriately and clearly in the final contract.

Execution and record keeping

Contracts made abroad are subject to the executive, legislative and judicial apparatus of the foreign nation. This submission gives the foreign country both territorial and extra-territorial jurisdiction over the domestic company, as we have suggested in earlier discussion. Sometimes the jurisdiction rises because of the 'presence' of the domestic company; other times because of its 'activities'; still other times from the express terms of the contract — and, in other cases, from the implied obligations that are read into it under the applicable statute, decree, judicial decision or custom and usage. In all instances, it is important that the negotiator see to the execution of the contract in compliance with the foreign law obtaining at the place where the contract was made. If he does not, his company could find itself in the position of being subject to the law of the foreign company while barred, because of an imperfectly executed contract, from invoking remedies and reliefs that would have been available to it were the contract perfect in form under the local requirements.

Assuming that all of the local legal requisites have been supplied, the negotiator should see to it that records, registration and filing are also accomplished in accordance with local practice and regulation. Procedurally, it is essential that the contract be given a valid inception — and this falls to the negotiator. He, of course can act through his local attorneys, or through company counsel, but the responsibility for satisfactory execution of the transactional papers remains with him. When he leaves the foreign country, he should be able to present the contract to his company free of any disabling omission or error. Partial compliance does not suffice. Nor should the ngeotiator place his company in an equivocal position in which it must pray the indulgence of the foreign company, or forgo its rights, merely because a test of legal validity and strength would assuredly find the domestic company incapable of pursuing its contractual rights.

Throughout every transaction abroad there is a dichotomous sense of distaste for detailed care, and along with it an uneasiness related to the foreign law. The best way to deal with the matter is to have every legal 'i' dotted and every 't' crossed in every word on every line of the contracting papers before they are signed by the negotiator.

Bi-lingual conformity

Whatever is reduced to contract must be clear; and the clarity should be stated in the contracting languages. Abstract words, technical phrases, standard terms, and polysyllabic words in either language can be rendered without twisting the meaning of the contract. The difficulties come to light when an article, a simple common word that may be used as a preposition or an adverb finds no equivalent in either of the languages. Chinese, for example, does not have articles; nor does Russian and doubtless other tongues. The emphatic English 'Are you going', 'Do you mean this', taken easily at home simply will not travel well. Other languages simply omit such forms. But the discussion on linguistics can be pursued elsewhere at the reader's option. It is enough to say that we think and speak one way; and how we think and speak cannot always be faithfully rendered by a linguistic equivalent abroad. Here then, as in all other phases of negotiating foreign contracts, the negotiator must actively assure himself that the contract phraseology is interchangeable, and equal in express and implied meaning, both factually and in regard to legal consequences.

There are translators and interpreters, philologists, etymologists, at home and abroad who have spent years in their specialities — and who still come up against perplexing words, most of them utterly simple and in common use, but having no exactly translatable parallel in another language. If such experts acknowledge this to be the case, it becomes obvious that the negotiator need not be too diffident about insisting on perfection in the rendition of what he has carefully carved out of the negotiation and placed into the final contract.

Nor will it suffice to get an approximation of wording. Admittedly, English is a richer language than many others, possibly than any other. Nevertheless, it is the foreign language that will govern the contract; and if it is narrower, if it is less flexible, if it is replete with oxymorons and deficient in workable synonyms, the responsibility still lies on the shoulders of the negotiator. If he has not appreciated the problem before, he can do so now. Think, for example, of the differences in meaning attached to 'wait', 'expect', 'anticipate', 'attend', 'abide' — and bear in mind that despite their differences, they all imply a common sense of looking forward to an impending event. How many foreign languages possess these synonyms? And, if they do not, should not the negotiator be even more careful of the contract's translation?

According to the number of parties to the foreign business, the negotiator ought to be careful in determining who is to receive copies, in what order, for what purpose, and whether such copies may be held permanently or returned, either to the official repository or to the designated notary. The need for preserving confidentiality speaks for itself; and the more carefully controlled the number of copies and the distribution, the safer the transaction's security. In order to confine the distribution of the copies to those alone authorized or empowered to act for the principles, a table of distribution should be agreed prior to the opening of the foreign negotiation.

There is another reason for limiting the distribution of copies of the contract and subsidiary papers. Foreign transactions involve foreign government offices and municipal bureaux. It may run contrary to national, or local policy there to distribute information that might be subject to official secrets acts. Improper, unauthorized or reckless disclosure of any kind can be dangerous and can lead to official enquiry abroad, with its attendant consequences. More importantly, it can jeopardize the principal purpose for entering the international matter: profit. A contract that leads to unpleasant notoriety, with the risk of arrest and conviction — accompanied by an invitation to leave the country in lieu of serving a prison sentence is not the ideal way to do foreign business. That this is not a speculative horror story can be verified by reading the numerous accounts of business men who have been caught up by careless dissemination of contract information abroad. The negotiator abroad needs a low profile. He also must protect his company from the zealous rivalry of its keen competitors. This makes it a first order of security for him to regulate and control the distribution of any and all copies of the memoranda, preliminary drafts and executed contracts. In the event that he has forgotten to do so, he should quickly repair the omission and do whatever else may be indicated as necessary to return himself and the domestic company to the good graces of the foreign powers that be. And, at the same time he does so he would be extremely foresighted if he renewed his friendly communications with the nearest consulate flying the flag of his native land.

Contract topics

Abroad as at home there are business considerations that affect every transaction, that ought to be dealt with, and that cannot be safely passed without risking loss, damage or injury.

The foreign negotiation at one time or other during its course runs into issues with plainly substantive matters; at other times, procedural questions must be met. Both branches of business problems are common in the domestic and foreign markets. But they are treated differently at contract time. To suggest them is enough to warn the negotiator that he must think of them from the foreign as well as from his own point of view. Each of the following topics are run of the mill, so to speak, as subjects for discussion. Yet each must be set within the foreign context, the foreign business practise, and, of course, the foreign language:

> Profitability; Risk; Exposure to loss; Damages; Liability; Recoupment; Escape clauses; Rescission; Reformation; Re-negotiation; Controversies and disputes; Intervention; Arbitration; Mediation; Conciliation Performance; Discharge; Violations; Annulment and cancellation; Renewals; Claims and demands; Offsets; Assignments and third parties; Warranties; Accommodations

The first topic can be illustrative of the approach needed for all of them. Thus, profitability, originally projected by the domestic company for a venture with a French cosmetic company at Paris, now must be calculated and provided for in order to compensate for the fluctuation of the English pound, (or the American dollar, or the Italian lira). The compensatory provision must be included in the contract; and, to be useful, it should supply the mechanism for preserving the projected profitability against radical movements in any of the relevant currencies, in relation to the French franc. Whether the negotiator prefers and can get his foreign adversary to agree to a sliding scale, or to a percentage or any other method is bound to be determined by prevailing market conditions; but the important point is this: profitability must be dealt with and insured against subsequent movements of money. The responsibility for doing so lies with the negotiator before he reaches final agreement. And the contract must express that provision in appropriate language.

Escape clauses, damage clauses and performance standards must, as with all other routine business issues, be treated as if they were special issues because, under foreign provisions, they do receive different constructions — and the negotiator must be certain that he achieves the precise provision his company requires for its protection under foreign law. One of the most difficult topics is 'notice'. At home it is burdensome enough; abroad it can be more than burdensome — it can vitiate the domestic company's rights unless the exact wording necessary to preserve them is contained in the contract. The nature of the notice, the time when it must be given, the party to whom it must be given, the place to which it must be sent, the manner in which it must be sent, and the wording it must contain cannot be assumed or presumed identical with the notice requirements in the domestic market. Whether the notice pertains to revocation or 'automatic renewals' (that often are not automatic), notice is a demanding topic and deserves as much care as any other contract provision to be agreed abroad.

Similarly, questions of assignment, recoupment and recovery, together with all of the indicated other topics, must be accepted as inviting contractual reconciliation with foreign law. In short, the ngeotiator cannot take as granted anything save the need to protect his company against misadventure.

Standard clauses

At home, standard clauses, commonly called 'boiler-plate' are in common, widespread and careless use. When the business goes well, no-one questions what they say or what they may mean. When the contracts become onerous, then everyone runs to a microscope to see how best to construe 'boiler-plate' into an escape hatch. Sometimes, by good luck, there is an inexpensive exit available. More often than not, the standard clause becomes a classic case of contractual rigor mortis, with an iron grip on the unfortunate party. International business also has a large variety of 'standard' clauses. But the negotiator must not be lulled into believing that they are any less deadly at the foreign site than they are at home. On the contrary, the language of the standard clauses must be read and understood literally and in conjunction with the foreign trade practices and customs and usages. For example, 'delivery' is so old a word at home and abroad that its inclusion in a standard clause might slip by unremarked. Yet the International Chamber of Commerce had to labour long and hard to define 'delivery' satisfactorily, so that it could express the kind of delivery that should be spelled out of the contract. Whether 'delivery' meant delivery to the foreign border, or to the indland transport service, or to the final destination may still be an open question, in spite of the efforts of the ICC and the explanations supplied in its glossary.

Nor is it sufficient to take a troublesome definition from the translator or interpreter. The negotiator must satisfy himself

that the word can be put to rest. Whether he does so by dictionary, his foreign lawyer's secretary, or otherwise, he must be right and he must be diligent. 'Delivery' is not always duty-paid delivery or door-to-door delivery, or delivery at buyer's cost. And the other ordinary contract words also have a chameleonic effect, taking their interpretation from the particular foreign place where they are used.
What should be done to avoid mistakes and damage?

1. Read and re-read all standard clauses
2. Take every doubtful word out; use an agreed equivalent, after verifying its propriety.
3. Reconcile the bi-lingual uses of the word.
4. Submit all uncertain usage to counsel.
5. Harmonize agreed terms with adversary, if possible.

In general, for easy reference, the negotiator should orient himself to a solid familiar meaning of business clauses in his own language. This will be a good point of departure for checking the foreign language equivalents. And it makes a safe operating procedural beginning. Thus, if he remembers that 'reservations' pertain to rights exercisable by the party who is given a specific option to do so, and *also* to rights by-passed by the negotiators, he will be able to cope with the substance and form of 'reservations' in the contract. To the same effect, see below:
Exclusions: Specifically barred topics, with or without explanation
Specifications: Technical particulars of some physical item or mechanical function, or recordable phenomenon
Particulars: Itemisation of properties, e.g. tensile strength
Quantity/quality descriptions: Number, grade, unit. incidence
Notice: Apprisal provided under law, contract, usage or custom for inception or termination of right, remedy or claim
Norms: Acceptable levels of proprietary characteristics or services within a social or economic structure, community.
Standards: Criteria for evaluation or performance (contractual)
Receipt: Acquisition of physical control of property of communication
Acceptance: Assent to contractual terms, condition of delivered property or services performed.
Terms: Statement of contractual rights and duties

Conditions: Events, contingencies and events governing contract

Incorporation by reference: Adoption of external information by identification not by text.

Payment: Exchange of money, things or services for acts done or to be done under contract

Papers: All principal and secondary written instruments forming final negotiated contract

Currency: Legal tender in general circulation at places designated in contract for payment, or otherwise

Reclamation: Right to seize goods provided by law or contract, on default or other breach of agreement.

Recapture: Similar to above, but includes all those claiming under derivative rights

General sources for referential materials, useful for verifying technical data, trade terms, consular regulations, economic conditions in foreign market, etc. can be found in the following:

1. Government publications
2. University, technical, business libraries
3. Industrial, commercial and mercantile reports
4. Standard commercial and industrial ratings
5. Credit ratings, classifications and reports
6. Trade association journals and house organs
7. Banking periodicals and journals
8. Academic special studies, seminars and reports
9. Economic community reports and releases
10. Trade and industrial union reports
11. Marketing journals
12. Management studies and reports
13. Shipping lists, port studies
14. Arbitration journals, association reports
15. Chamber of commerce, local and international
16. Industrial and market, economic surveys
17. Press releases, news reports, special feature items
18. Consular representatives, at home and abroad
19. Tribunal reports of litigation, at home and abroad
20. Legal, accounting and engineering specialists oriented toward international transactions

There is no intention on the part of the author to suggest that the foregoing is adequate as a list of available material. But it can stimulate the reader to enquiries that he might not have included in his original research for background or other kinds of materials. It need not be said too strongly that the negotiator's personal contacts abroad, official and unofficial, can be extremely helpful in locating office-archives and other places where records not generally available to the public might be pursued. Each negotiator may have a special requirement for information, whether it is technical, cultural or scientific, before he goes abroad he ought to know where to go and whom to see in order to get a sight of the desired documents, books, records, notes, memoranda or other papers that have a bearing on the foreign business that he intends to accomplish. In many foreign countries information is closely guarded, difficult to get at, and not accessible at convenient hours — if at all.

It will be assumed that the negotiator will by this time have an appreciation of the need for taking opinion of counsel on all points related to the foreign business. Nevertheless, the negotiator must always ask himself whether he ought to have the contract executed at the site of the negotiation or at his home office. Advantages to his company vary with the place of contract. And sometimes the foreign jurisdiction affords wider scope for the domestic company — as, for example with regard to tax benefits.

If he can settle the practical aspect of superior or inferior legal considerations, that is to say those that touch his company's interests, he can leave legal theory concerning the law of the place where the contract was made and the law of the place where it will be performed to his legal experts, at the home office or in the foreign country. The topic, international law, is difficult, and adds nothing to the skill of the negotiations; it is enough for him to pass it on to the legal department of his company. But so far as the attachment of foreign jurisdiction, he should remember that his company as well as its negotiators can become subject to foreign jurisdiction in at least a dozen or more instances, many of which are only barely connected with his 'physical presence' in the place. In fact, in some instances, even if he does not go into the foreign jurisdiction at all, his domestic company can be declared the subject of foreign proceedings in the foreign courts, or before foreign administrative bodies.

He should also remember that arbitration is not uniform everywhere. Arbitrations may be held under agreement, by participation without prior agreement, by operation of law as provided in statute; and each country has its own arbitration forums and procedural regulations. Conciliation is another form of quasi-judicial or extra-judicial intervention. And like arbitration it varies in form from country to country. The same may be said of mediation. The point to be retained is that merely providing for any of these three proceedings can be dangerous where the negotiator does not know the local form. He cannot rely on his experience of these three non-litigational methods at home as a guide to what they will look like abroad.

More importantly, he cannot take for granted the personal integrity of arbitrators, conciliators or mediators abroad. He should know something more about the likelihood of panel proceedings as distinguished from individual intervention before he commits his company.

Any doubt as to his ability to get a fair hearing for his company at an arbitration, should be resolved against the acceptance of such a proceeding, if the negotiator has the choice of proceeding available to him.

Furthermore, the rendering of a decision after arbitration, or conciliation or mediation may not be an end in itself. Further proceedings may be required abroad to give the decision the effect of a judicial decree, with teeth in it sufficient to let the negotiator's company benefit by its provisions. As to arbitration, the ngeotiator ought to discuss its merits with company counsel before he elects to agree to foreign arbitration.

This is a rough resumé of the points to be settled:

1. Contract provisions for arbitration
2. What is an arbitrable dispute?
3. How is dispute submitted for arbitration
4. How are arbitrators designated?
5. How are issues presented?
6. What proof is admissable?
7. How are time, place and date for arbitration fixed?
8. What are non-arbitrable issues?
9. What does the arbitrator do during the hearing, after the evidence is in, and in deciding the case?
10. How is a decision, and how is an award, rendered?

11. What must be done to confirm each of them?
12. What is the legal effect of each?
13. What are the rights of appeal?
14. Who may appeal?
15. What rights exist to enforce the award and the judgment entered on it?
16. Where may the judgment be enforced?
17. Are arbitration judgments supported by additional remedies?

The foregoing elements are conventional necessities at home. They should be raised, considered and answered with respect to foreign negotiations before the negotiator commits himself to a position that may result in a waiver of his company's rights to litigate in a formal tribunal.